MORE PRAISE FOR
ON LEADERSHIP

"Dr. Palmisano has provided a compelling analysis of the road to STERLING leadership and how it can be attained. His advice and guidance, along with words of encouragement for perseverance, provide the reader with a sensible understanding of the many contributing factors which certify the acquisition of real leadership."

—Edward Annis, MD,
AMA President, 1963–64

"Donald Palmisano's dissection of the components and attributes of leadership identifies some of the most critical and often overlooked elements, namely the essential role that personal courage and persistence play in outstanding leaders. His use of real life examples transforms what would otherwise be dry abstract thoughts into tangible, reality-based lessons."

—Jim Bagian, MD, P.E.,
Director, National Center for Patient Safety and Chief Patient Safety Officer for Veterans Health Administration, U.S. Department of Veterans Affairs

"Donald Palmisano has awed and inspired audiences for years. *On Leadership* transforms into written word his unequalled power to inspire and motivate. A must read for any aspiring leader!"

—Patti Herlihy,
AMA Alliance President, 2002–03

"I am enthused to learn Dr. Palmisano's thoughts about leadership based on his substantial experiences and Leadership roles in the two fields of medicine and law. He has recognized not only the role of leaders but also the collateral position as follower, a responsibility leaders do not often see for themselves. His use of specific experiences to make clear the attributes of leaders and leadership are valuable and clarifying contributions to his thoughts."

—Robert D. Sparks, MD,
President and Chief Programming Officer, W. K.
Kellogg Foundation (*Retired*)

"I couldn't put this book down. Its true stories exemplifying leadership are compelling and engrossing. They clearly and logically lead to lessons that painlessly can boost your leadership skills. Whether you are in the catbird seat or you'd like to be, you'll benefit from reading Donald Palmisano's seminal lessons about leadership."

—Dr. Gwynn Akin Bowers,
Vice President, Syntex Corporation (*Retired*)

"A magnificent outpouring of the truths learned by the careful observations of a questioning mind."

—Ronald J. French, MD,
Reigned as Rex, King of New Orleans Mardi Gras in 2007

ON LEADERSHIP

ON LEADERSHIP

ESSENTIAL PRINCIPLES
FOR SUCCESS

Donald J. Palmisano

Foreword by
Bobby Jindal
Governor of Louisiana

SKYHORSE PUBLISHING

Skyhorse Publishing books may be purchased in bulk at special
discounts for sales promotion, corporate gifts, fund raising, or
educational purposes. Special editions can also be created to
specifications. For details, contact Special Sales Department,
Skyhorse Publishing, 555 Eighth Avenue, Suite 903,
New York, NY 10018 or info@skyhorsepublishing.com.

www.skyhorsepublishing.com

10 9 8 7 6 5 4 3 2 1

Library of Congress Cataloging-in-Publication Data

Palmisano, Donald J.
   On leadership : essential principles for success / Donald
Palmisano.
      p. cm.
   Includes bibliographical references and index.
   ISBN 978-1-60239-321-9 (alk. paper)
   1. Leadership. 2. Success—Psychological aspects. I. Title.

BF637.L4P35 2008
158'.4—dc22   2008012881

Printed in China

This book is dedicated to my grandchildren, youngest to the oldest: Pablo, Diego, Alexis, Marco, Ryan, and Brittany. They are a constant source of joy for their Nana and me. My hope is that this book will serve as a North Star for leadership in their generation. As the grandchildren review this text in the years ahead, my efforts will be doubly rewarded if they reflect fondly on their practice speech sessions with Paw Paw as they delivered their version of "Do your homework, have courage, and don't give up! Words mean something; actions have consequences!" I thank them for all of the love and wonderful memories.

—*DJP 2008*

CONTENTS

FOREWORD

As we know all too well in my home state of Louisiana, strong leadership, or a lack thereof, can affect the lives of thousands. The world watched in horror following the landfall of Hurricane Katrina, as leadership at seemingly every level broke down and failed the people of the Gulf Coast.

At a time when leadership was needed most, so many failed to step up to the cause. We heard every excuse in the book as to why help did not arrive in a timely manner, or as to why food, water, and other supplies could not get to those who needed it most. It is at times like these when a leader must step up, risk the consequences, and push forward without excuses. Indeed, in contrast with the bureaucracy, many churches, businesses, Coast Guard and National Guard members, sheriff's deputies, volunteers, and many others did not worry about permission or credit, and instead did what had to be done to save lives.

However, leadership often manifests itself on a smaller scale, but with consequences just as important. Be it someone with the courage to stand up in the face of oppression, or with the heart and compassion to help those less fortunate, leaders play a vital role in our everyday lives.

Too often however, those with the capability to lead lose sight of what is important, be it for wealth, fame, or any other number of things. As Dr. Donald Palmisano notes in this very book, there is a significant difference between achieving success and being a leader. In fact, many times leaders must sacrifice their own personal goals and dreams in order to help those around them.

I have known Donald for quite a few years now, and feel confident in saying that he exemplifies many qualities befitting a leader. Learning lessons from his father, a New Orleans police officer, he has built himself into not only a successful surgeon and businessman, but a strong leader as well.

You will read a quote from me later in this book about what it means to be a leader, as well as the thoughts of many other accomplished professionals. I can only hope that you take some of these thoughts and ideas to heart, and become a leader in your own right.

—Governor Bobby Jindal
State of Louisiana

INTRODUCTION

Again and again, an enlightened and strong-willed
individual has pushed against the prevailing trends
and the prevailing wisdom to perform an act of courage that has changed history.
  —Paul Johnson, "Needed: Leaders of Courage"
                              Forbes, May 7, 2007

Leaders make decisions that make events happen.
Obviously there is more to the definition of leadership, as tyrants do the same and they are not leaders.
Many books on leadership offer success stories as a
way of saying, "This is leadership and this is what I
did to achieve it." Unfortunately, those books do not
clarify that success alone does not equal leadership.
Some of the authors also imply that all of the steps
they took toward their success are necessary for others to follow. In many cases, some of their actions
had nothing to do with their receiving an honor or a
position as CEO of a company.

Effective leadership can be taught. This book
focuses on the essential elements of true leadership.
Think of it as identifying the critical DNA of leadership, akin to the twenty percent of the DNA of

a human genome that accounts for the characteristics of the individual, the other eighty percent being "junk DNA" or noncoding DNA.

Here in this book are a set of proven, simple-to-follow steps to becoming a leader and achieving success through essential principles taken from my personal experiences and observations. This starts from acknowledging that success and leadership are not the same. I identify ways of avoiding or overcoming such roadblocks as wasted effort, false starts, and disappointments. And I'll illustrate each of these principles with an example of people who have demonstrated exceptional qualities—courage, persistence, intelligence, strength of character, etc.—through their actions, their personal philosophies, or their writings. Many of these leaders personally shared with me their definition of leadership for this book and these exemplary figures together help to set standards for anyone who aspires to a leadership position. Along with an analysis of practical methods or strategies of leadership, each chapter ends with a list of "Lessons Learned," highlighting what I'd like you to take away from reading each chapter.

As I explain in chapter 1, before and after Hurricane Katrina state and local officials were exposed as too incompetent or too weak to confront critical problems and make lifesaving decisions. Understandably, leadership ability was in the forefront of the minds of Louisiana voters in the 2007 gubernatorial election. And it certainly ought to be on the minds of American voters in all presidential and congressional elections.

The twenty-first century has shown that terrorism can make our own corner of the world a dangerous place. Democracy and liberty thrive when we identify true leaders and nurture potential ones. I encourage you to read and enjoy the book, to pursue leadership skills, and to seek out true leaders. Our survival—yours and mine—may depend on it.

CHAPTER 1

THE ANTITHESIS
OF LEADERSHIP

Be willing to make decisions. That's the most important quality in a good leader. Don't fall victim to what I call the "ready-aim-aim-aim-aim syndrome." You must be willing to fire.

—General George S. Patton, Jr.

During the final weekend of August 2005, millions of people along the northern coast of the Gulf of Mexico held their collective breath as Hurricane Katrina, one of modern history's most powerful storms, approached landfall. By Saturday, August 27, Katrina seemed poised to score a direct hit on the city of New Orleans.

The following morning, at 10:11 a.m., the National Weather Service office in New Orleans issued a message marked "URGENT." "Devastating damage expected," the message read,

> Hurricane Katrina, a most powerful hurricane with unprecedented strength, rivaling the intensity of Hurricane Camille of 1969 ... Most of the [New Orleans] area will be uninhabitable for weeks, perhaps longer. ... All wood-framed, low-rising apartment buildings will be destroyed. ... All gabled roofs will fail. ... High-rise office and apartment buildings will sway dangerously. ... Airborne debris will be widespread. And may include heavy items such as household appliances and even light vehicles. Sport utility vehicles and light trucks will be moved. Water shortages will make human suffering incredible by modern standards. ... The vast majority of native trees will be snapped or uprooted. Only the heartiest will remain standing, but will be totally defoliated.[1]

When Hurricane Katrina raged its way ashore in the pre-dawn hours of Monday, August 29, its center was miles outside of New Orleans's eastern boundary. As darkness gave way to daylight, the weather bureau's predictions proved to be somewhat off the mark. Hurricane-force winds and rain had indeed wrought major damage from one end of town to the other. But the city had escaped the apocalyptic events that were forecast.

During the three previous days, about three quarters of New Orleans's population fled to inland points in all directions but south. By Monday midmorning, families in hotel rooms from Houston to Dallas and Memphis readied themselves to return home, eager to discover how their residences and businesses had fared.

Shortly before noon, five or six hours after the hurricane left the city, television and radio reports announced a new crisis. Along Lake Pontchartrain, which forms New Orleans's northern boundary, levees were giving way. In a matter of hours, five breaks in three levees submerged seventy-five percent of the city. In some places the depths reached eight feet or more.

By early afternoon hundreds of people were walking through the inner city in chest-high water, desperately looking for higher ground. Hundreds more were washed away in the streets. Many of those who stayed in their homes or managed to find their way back had to climb into attics to escape the water and then hack their way to the rooftops. Some perished in their attics. Others died on their roofs, from exposure or hunger or both.

They were among the multitude of New Orleanians, many of them poor, who had chosen to ride out the storm. Their reasons varied: About one hundred thousand residents had no means of personal transportation, or the money to get it. Others were too old or feeble to risk an arduous trip. Many wanted to protect their possessions from post-hurricane thieves and vandals. Still others couldn't face the prospect of evacuation, which could mean hundreds of miles of slow-moving traffic and fuel shortages.

Substituting Excuses for Leadership

I was born in Louisiana. I've spent almost my entire life there. And I believe that a sizeable number of those who stayed had acquired over the years a kind of go-it-alone attitude when forced to make a possible life or death choice. Where did this attitude come from? Many no doubt read and listened to one account after another demonstrating that their local and state officials could not be trusted when the time came for critical decision making.

New Orleans Mayor Ray Nagin issued the evacuation order twenty hours before Katrina struck the Louisiana coast—less than half the time researchers determined would be needed to get everyone out. According to one expert in transportation planning who had helped the city put together its evacuation plan, city officials had 550 municipal buses and hundreds of additional school buses at their disposal, but had made no plans to use them to get people out. One high-ranking city employee later reported that the school buses couldn't be used because they were partly submerged and the keys to start them couldn't be found. The mayor's excuse was that drivers weren't available, meaning that the city's emergency planners failed to commit them in advance.[2]

On Thursday, September 1, the fourth day after the hurricane struck, Michael D. Brown, director of the Federal Emergency Management Agency (FEMA), revealed to CNN's Paula Zahn that government officials had not been aware for days that—besides the hurricane victims stranded in the Louisiana Superdome—thousands more had taken refuge in the New Orleans Convention Center about a mile away:

> **Brown:** "And so, this—this catastrophic disaster continues to grow. I will tell you this, though. Every person in that convention center, *we just learned about that today*. And so, I have directed that we have all available resources to get to that convention center to make certain that they have the food and water, the medical care that they need."
> **Zahn:** "Sir, you aren't telling me ..."
> **Brown:** "... and that we take care of those bodies that are there."
> **Zahn:** "Sir, you aren't telling me you just learned that the folks at the convention center didn't have food and water until today, are you? You had no idea they were completely cut off?"

Brown: "Paula, the federal government did not even know about the convention center people until today."

Later, Brown would say he was wrong, and that FEMA actually knew about the victims at the convention center twenty-four hours earlier but was unable to reach them until Thursday.[3]

Could anyone have anticipated and planned for this crisis? The need for timely evacuation, transport of those who could not help themselves, and the risk of flooding in the below sea-level bowl that is New Orleans had been clearly spelled out in 2004, the year before Katrina struck, in a three-day-long practice scenario named "Hurricane Pam."[4] The purpose of that exercise, which focused on a hypothetical hurricane similar to Katrina in its effect, was to develop a recovery plan for the thirteen parishes (the Louisiana equivalent of counties) in the New Orleans area. It involved more than 250 emergency preparedness officials from more than fifty federal, state and local agencies and volunteer organizations. A FEMA press release of July 23, 2004, had this to say about the hypothetical Hurricane Pam:

> "We made great progress this week in our preparedness efforts," said Ron Castleman, FEMA Regional Director. "Disaster response teams developed action plans in critical areas such as search and rescue,

medical care, sheltering, temporary housing, school restoration and debris management. These plans are essential for quick response to a hurricane but will also help in other emergencies."[5]

Yet a year later, no one in the corridors of power appeared to have heeded the report's distinct and repeated warnings. Chairman Tom Davis of the Congressional Select Bipartisan Committee to Investigate the Preparation for and Response to Hurricane Katrina said on December 15, 2005, at the Hearing on Preparedness and Response in Louisiana, "[Hurricane Exercise] Pam was so very prescient. And yet Katrina highlighted many, many weaknesses that either were not anticipated by Pam, or were lessons learned but not heeded. That's probably the most painful thing about Katrina, and the tragic loss of life: the foreseeability of it all." The Select Committee stated in the executive summary:

The Select Committee identified failures at all levels of government that significantly undermined and detracted from the heroic efforts of first responders, private individuals and organizations, faith-based groups, and others. ... The institutional and individual failures we have identified became all the more clear compared to the heroic efforts of those who acted decisively. Those who didn't flinch, who took matters into their own hands when bureaucratic inertia was causing death, injury, and suffering. Those whose exceptional initiative saved time and money and lives.[6]

Leadership Versus Opportunism

Anyone can pass for a leader in a problem-free world. Many people in positions of power perform quite capably in the absence of controversy or danger. True leaders emerge when a crisis has to be confronted, when an important problem has to be assessed, and decisive action has to be taken.

Philosopher George Santayana said in *Reason in Common Sense*, "Those who cannot remember the past are condemned to repeat it." Yet in the case of public officials, we see the same failures by people who were elected to lead but instead repeat and even compound the errors of their predecessors. Too often in present day politics events are allowed to unfold without the critical intervention needed to save the day. What is the reason for this recurrent problem? Is it that voters choose the candidate who panders to them the most?

There is probably no limit to the different ways officeholders can abdicate their leadership responsibilities. One common example is role reversal, in which someone who was chosen to lead instead becomes a follower.

Evaluating a political candidate's leadership potential is difficult in an environment where a candidate's core principles have to take a backseat to polling and survey results. Too many candidates delay their decisions on issues until the poll numbers are known. Perhaps a variation of the following imaginary conversation takes place in many a campaign:

Candidate: "What do the poll numbers show?"

Campaign manager: "They show that sixty-two percent favor the construction of a levee closer to the water's edge."

Candidate: "Then I'll advocate that position in my keynote speech tonight."

Campaign manager: "But the nonpartisan scientific panel found that the soil in that area will not support a levee."

Candidate: "Find other individuals with degrees behind their names who support the poll's position. Let's not be foolish here. Who knows where the truth lies? We must represent the people."

The most generous argument one can make for this candidate is that he or she can at least make a decision.

Dante Alighieri, the thirteenth-century Italian poet and writer, defines this personality dramatically in his *Divine Comedy*. Among the scoundrels populating Dante's *Inferno* is a group of souls, "The Opportunists," in the Vestibule of Hell who had refused to take sides in battle. These scoundrels spend their time in hell scurrying to and fro, chasing a blank banner, avoiding decisions and willing to accept any value system rather than adhere to a single set of valid core principles. Dante shows his particular disdain for these Opportunists by having them continually suffer the stings of hornets.

More than two and a half years after the hurricane, issues critical to New Orleans's poststorm recovery are still being debated. In fact, problems that date back to 1965, when Hurricane Betsy ravaged the city, still haven't been addressed by those chosen to lead.

In September 1965, the day after Betsy struck New Orleans, the city's mayor broadcast an emergency request stating that any available doctor should report to City Hall. I responded to the call, and when I arrived at the mayor's office he handed me a piece of paper with an address written on it. "Rush to this storm shelter," he said. "People need medical help now."

At the shelter I found about 2,000 people, many in dire need of care. One was a diabetic woman who had no supply of vital insulin.

I asked one of the volunteers where the medical supplies were. "There are none," was the answer.

"Where's the telephone?" I asked. "There is no phone," I was told.

During the four plus decades that have elapsed since Hurricane Betsy, I've found very little change in the city's ability to respond effectively in a major disaster.

In the aftermath of Katrina, severed communication was once again blamed for delayed assistance and widespread human suffering. As soon as I realized communications were dismal because of lack of preparation, I managed to obtain donations of communications equipment and began distributing them to other physicians helping to provide disaster relief.

By November of 2007, more than two years after Katrina, state government had distributed at least twenty-eight "interoperable radios" to each parish, according to parish officials. But the state had yet to establish uniform procedures for their use during a disaster. One Louisiana sheriff complained that twenty-eight radios per parish were not nearly enough to link all the local first responders on call during disasters. He added, "There is no control policy on what channels or whatever to use. We're spending tons of money on structure, but we still can't communicate."[7]

Meanwhile, tens—perhaps hundreds—of thousands of New Orleanians were still waiting for government officials to decide or take action on storm-related issues crucial to their return to normal lives—issues like removing debris, controlling crime, providing an adequate water supply, and repairing badly damaged streets. Serious doubts remained that governments at all levels were prepared to deal effectively with another similar disaster.

Decisiveness is Critical

In the months following Katrina, citizens, state and federal officials, engineers and other experts wrangled over the issue of improving the levee systems in Louisiana's coastal areas. Citizens and interest groups were demanding a restructuring of the state's various regional "levee boards," whose members oversaw the maintenance of the water-retaining structures.

The backpedaling and dawdling coming from the governor's office in December 2005 prompted James Gill, a columnist at the New Orleans daily newspaper, *The Times-Picayune*, to comment:

> Today Gov. Kathleen Blanco is in favor of levee board reform, but yesterday she seemed intent on scuttling it. Earlier it seemed she couldn't care less. Where she will stand tomorrow is a matter of speculation. So insistent has been the public clamor for reform that Blanco was finally forced to take her fingers out of her ears. … Blanco has been in politics long enough to have a sense of the voters' mood. Ever since Katrina, everyone has been waiting for her to do something—anything. Instead, it seemed we were in for more procrastination and another retreat from the fray.[8]

Needlessly delaying or agonizing over decisions is not leadership. World War II's General George Patton correctly identified decisiveness as a critical element in being an effective leader.

Michael Bloomberg is a public official who knows what Patton is talking about. His first election as mayor of New York came two months after the attack on that city's World Trade Center on September 11, 2001. During his second term he took his first tour of the devastation that Hurricane Katrina had inflicted on New Orleans. At one point during the tour he stopped to say, "I'm not here to brag about New York. You know New Yorkers are famously modest and shy," he quipped. "But our recovery didn't happen by accident. It happened because we did what we were hired to do: to lead and to manage for results."[9]

Those final two sentences of Bloomberg's statement are what leadership is all about.

Lessons Learned

- The flawed or insufficient responses to the devastation in New Orleans from Hurricane Katrina is a textbook example of a lack of leadership.
- Leadership is not indecision. It is not procrastination. It is not disorganization. It is not lack of preparation. Leaders are not missing in action. Leaders are visible and make decisions in emergencies with the information available.

- False leaders are everywhere during times of calm, and then are inept and indecisive in an emergency.
- To prevent future failures, past failures must be studied. Lessons learned must be implemented.

CHAPTER 2

ADVICE FROM THE PAST: FOUNDATION OF SUCCESS

Danger invites rescue; the cry of distress is the summons to relief.

—Judge Benjamin Cardozo, 1921

Some years ago, on a steamy August day in New Orleans, police rushed to a bungalow in a middle-income neighborhood, where a troubled man held several hostages at gunpoint.

Arriving at the scene, the squad cars clustered near the curb as the man watched from a window. He held a gun to the head of one of the hostages.

Once the police assessed the situation, the ranking officer had to come up with a tactic that would avoid bloodshed. Storming the house was out of the question. A lengthy standoff could intensify matters and increase the dangers the hostages faced.

The officer reached a decision. He opened the door of his car and got out. Then he approached the house slowly—yet steadfastly—as the gunman looked on.

Midway between the curb and the front door of the house, the officer stopped. He removed his coat, took the service revolver from his holster, and laid the weapon on the ground. Then, even more slowly, almost casually, he walked through the door and up to the hostage taker. The distance between the unarmed policeman and the gunman was no more than a few feet.

The man pointed his weapon at the policeman's face and said, "Now I'm gonna kill you."

Almost immediately the officer—calm and self-assured—raised his right hand. The gesture's purpose was not to ward off the weapon or to strike a blow. It was to feel the hostage taker's forehead.

"You have a fever," the policeman said. "Let me take you to a hospital."

Perhaps it was the shock effect of this sympathetic proposal that caused the gunman to change his mind. After a pause, he gave up his weapon and the policeman, true to his promise, personally took him to a hospital.

The hostages were unharmed and their lives were saved. The officer who defused the situation was my dad, Major Dominic Palmisano of the New Orleans Police Department.

The side of life that my father experienced in law enforcement was far different from the New Orleans of popular myth, the place often called "the city that care forgot." The city historically has had more than its share of violent crime, along with a police department long known for its internal discipline problems. Yet through all such pressures and demands, Dad remained a rock of integrity and a constant source of wisdom to many. People respected him, and counted on him. I know I did.

During my first year of medical school, with its unrelenting demands on my time and the need for dedication, I became discouraged. I questioned whether it was within me to succeed as a doctor. But Dad had confidence in me. He told me that one way to succeed in life was to follow a simple rule: "Do your homework, have courage and don't give up." This is a formula for success stripped to its essence.

I heeded those words. I stayed in school, and in 1963 I received my MD degree.

"Do your homework, have courage—and don't give up." Simple words. But powerful instructions to meet almost any challenge.

• • •

In the incident involving the hostage taker my father proved he lived by his own rule: He showed that by taking his police training seriously, he had done the homework required of somebody in his profession; that this training armed him with the courage to willingly confront an extremely dangerous situation, and that he was determined to avoid failure.

Some forty years later, when I was inaugurated as president of the American Medical Association, I told the doctors of America, "Tonight I commend this advice to you as we, as an organization, confront the threats to our profession and to the patients we swear an oath to serve. And I, too, take those words to heart tonight as I accept your charge as president of the AMA: Do your homework, have courage—and don't give up."

I firmly believe that my father's words of encouragement to me are relevant to anyone who strives for success in any venture. Doing the homework needed in any worthwhile effort will arm one with the basic resources needed to succeed. Having the courage to face the challenges they'll meet along the way will reinforce their self-confidence and attract the confidence of others. And the chances of failure will decrease when someone has the fierce determination to shake off distractions and obstacles by staying focused on success.

But there is a difference between success and leadership. A person attaining success is not necessarily a leader. My dad had a successful outcome to his story and he also was a leader. With words he taught me the secrets of success; by his actions he taught me the essentials of leadership.

Lessons Learned

- A crisis frequently can test one's courage.
- The commitment to "Do your homework, have courage—and don't give up" is vital to anyone seeking success.
- This advice is also important to leadership but success alone does not equal leadership.

CHAPTER 3

THE ESSENTIALS OF LEADERSHIP: SUCCESS CORNERSTONES AND MORE

Unbounded courage and compassion join'd,
Tempering each other in the victor's mind,
Alternately proclaim him good and great,
And make the hero and the man complete.

—Joseph Addison, *Campaign*, 1704

The young soldier led the charge on the battle-field. His horse was shot. He leaped onto the horse of a dead soldier and continued. Bullets pierced his clothes and his second horse was killed. He kept his cool and climbed on a third horse, rallying his troops.[1]

The Indian chief then told his braves, "Do not fire anymore at him. We waste bullets. He is protected by the Great Spirit."[2]

In future struggles against a stronger enemy, he lost battle after battle. Yet he never gave up. His leadership finally turned the tide of the war for independence from the British: On December 26, 1776, after leading his troops across the Delaware River in a storm, George Washington defeated the mercenaries fighting with the British at Trenton.

In a funeral oration for Washington, Congress selected a Virginia congressman and former Continental officer, Henry "Light Horse" Lee, to deliver the eulogy. He said of Washington, "First in war, first in peace, and first in the hearts of his countrymen."

Washington led from the front after getting the opinions of his colleagues about the planned attack. Once he did his homework, he chose the plan and led the attack. His soldiers loved and revered him. After the war, he refused offers to rule and returned to his farm in 1783, much like the Roman General Cincinnatus.

George Washington, who later became the first president of the United States, embodied leadership. But what are the essential qualities that made him such a great leader?

A person attaining success is not necessarily a leader; however, successful leadership requires incorporation of the foundations of success: homework, courage, and persistence.

Defining Leadership

The critical starting point for understanding leadership is identifying its essentials.

A true leader:

- does the necessary "homework."
- demonstrates courage.
- is persistent; doesn't give up when faced with challenges; is relentless in pursuit of goal.
- fully understands both the mission and the goal.
- has integrity; is ethical.
- is decisive.
- does not fail to act in the absence of either instructions for an unexpected crisis or the desired data on which to base decisions.
- is a good listener and an effective communicator.
- does not depend on the approval of others to build self-esteem.
- understands that unity leads to success and division leads to failure.
- leads "from the front."
- inspires others and engages them using his or her passion and authentic behavior.
- never asks others to take risks that he or she would not take.
- does not get rattled in a crisis.

- seeks opportunities to advance the mission.
- knows how to identify those who are sincere in interpersonal relations.
- is trustworthy and learns quickly whom to trust.
- is dependable, adhering to a company's or a movement's mission without compromising principles for personal enrichment or benefit.
- becomes a loyal follower and supporter of other leaders once they are identified.
- recognizes that leadership is not an ego trip.

Crisis as an Incubator of Leaders

Throughout history, the greatest leaders have emerged in the midst of crisis. No document provides clearer evidence of exceptional bravery—and outstanding leadership—than the citation issued to a member of the military when the U.S. government awards the Medal of Honor. The medal is given for "Conspicuous Gallantry and Intrepidity Involving Risk of Life Above and Beyond the Call of Duty in Action With the Enemy."

These awardees believe in the goals they set out to accomplish. While acting heroically to accomplish their mission, they put themselves at risk of death, and in many cases sacrifice their lives, in order to save others.

General Douglas MacArthur described a true leader as someone who has "the confidence to stand alone, the courage to make tough decisions, and the compassion to listen to the needs of others. He does not set out to be a leader, but becomes one by the equality of his actions and the integrity of his intent."[3]

Audie Murphy: A great example of a true leader is that of Lieutenant Audie Murphy, the most decorated combat soldier in World War II. The Medal of Honor citation he received in 1945 states that, facing six enemy tanks and "large numbers of advancing enemy infantry," Murphy climbed onto a burning U.S. Army tank destroyer armed with a .50-caliber machine gun. Alone and exposed to enemy fire from three sides, he managed to kill "dozens of Germans" and, ignoring a leg wound, continued to single-handedly fight for more than an hour, until his ammunition was exhausted. He returned to his company and, after refusing medication, led his men in a counterattack that forced the Germans to withdraw.

The citation states that Murphy's "indomitable courage and his refusal to give an inch of ground saved his company from possible encirclement and destruction, and enabled it to hold the woods which had been the enemy's objective."[4]

Here's what the citation doesn't say: Audie Murphy still had his telephone with him when he was on top of that burning tank destroyer firing the machine gun. The command post wanted to know how far away the enemy was. "Hold the phone and I'll let you talk to one of the bastards." Murphy replied.[5] He pointed the phone receiver toward a German who was climbing up the tank destroyer and then shot the man before he could be shot himself.

These actions dramatically illustrate the leadership quality of not getting rattled in a near-death situation. The world is hungry for heroes and leaders. Some of them often are living quietly among us, and their leadership skills go unnoticed until an emergency arises.

Wesley Autrey: On January 4, 2007, Wesley Autrey, a New York City construction worker and Vietnam veteran, performed a stunning act of heroism. He happened to be standing on the platform of a Manhattan subway station with his two daughters when he saw a young man, a student, fall backward and begin convulsing. As his daughters looked on, Autrey bent over the student and tried to clear his breathing passages. Then the young man stood up and stumbled, falling from the platform onto the subway train tracks below.

"I had a split-second decision to make," Autrey said later. "Do I let the train run him over and hear my daughters screaming and see the blood? Or do I jump in?"

He decided to act. "I dove in and I pinned him down," Autrey said. "The only thing that popped into my mind was go into the gutter [a trough between the track's rails]. Once the first [subway] car ran over us, then my thing was to keep him still."[6]

Autrey said the train that had passed above them "was probably two inches off my back." (The actual distance from the top of the rails to the lowest equipment beneath the subway car was two-and-three-quarters inches. The troughs below the tracks can be eight to twenty-four inches deep.)[7]

After the two men were lifted back onto the platform, the student was brought to a hospital for treatment of bumps and bruises. Autrey was not injured.

Heroes like Audie Murphy and Wesley Autrey aren't born every day. And very few leaders are called on to perform the kind of life-or-death bravery they displayed. But these two men's remarkable ability to perform in a crisis, to decide without delay and to act on that decision when action was called for, should be an example to everyone who aspires to be a leader.

Lessons Learned

- The cornerstones of success are homework, courage, and persistence, but leadership requires that and more: integrity, decisiveness, communication, and inspiration, to name only a few.
- A leader is defined as a fully informed and decisive person with integrity who advances

courageously toward a goal, and is determined to overcome obstacles and setbacks along the way.

- Sometimes a crisis tests a leader's ability to decide without delay, and to act on that decision when action is called for.

CHAPTER 4

A PRIMER ON "HOMEWORK"

A little learning is a dangerous thing; drink deep, or taste not the Pierian spring: there shallow draughts intoxicate the brain, and drinking largely sobers us again.

—Alexander Pope, *An Essay on Criticism*, 1709

In 1849 thousands of people in English cities were dying horrific deaths. In the Soho district of London alone the toll reached more than 14,000 lives. In the port city of Liverpool, more than 5,000 people were eventually struck down, and the Yorkshire town of Hull was to lose more than 1,800 inhabitants, a tragic number for a population of its size.

The killer was *Vibrio cholerae*, the microbe that causes cholera. Cholera produces severe watery diarrhea and vomiting, and it causes dehydration and death in thirty to fifty percent of untreated cases.[1] At the time, the prevailing view among physicians and scientists was that the spread of cholera and other infectious diseases originated in what the Greeks called miasma—polluted or noxious air. It was a theory that had first taken hold during the Middle Ages. Germ theory had yet to emerge.

One London physician practicing during this period, John Snow, was skeptical of the miasma theory, and, ultimately, the experiment he conducted in trying to justify his skepticism would change the course of medical history and create the profession of epidemiology.

Snow was convinced that contaminated water was the transmitter of the deadly germ, and the epidemic of 1848–49 prompted him to write his first treatise on the subject. His 1849 essay, *On the Mode of Communication of Cholera*, directly challenged the polluted-air theory.

Snow was a steel-willed man, the son of a coal yard worker whose monumental accomplishments went largely unrecognized in his own lifetime. Among his detractors were his own colleagues in the medical profession. This didn't discourage him. He knew he had carefully done his homework, and his determination never wavered.

Four years after the 1848–49 pestilence ended, a second outbreak of cholera brought more suffering to the English. The epidemic of 1853–54, which struck once again in London's Soho district, turned out to be worse than the previous one. It also provided Snow the opportunity to fully test his conviction that air was not a factor in spreading the disease.

In the earlier epidemic, the Soho neighborhood received water from two companies, both of which got it from the River Thames, which contained virtually all of the rubbish and filth produced by the world's then most heavily populated city.[2]

However, some time before the outbreak of 1853–54, one of the two companies began drawing water from a well with water that contained no traces of contamination from the river.

The existence of these two different water sources for Soho's population—one contaminated by sewage and the other free from contamination—presented a nearly ideal framework on which Snow could map out cholera cases based on the two sources. "I resolved to spare no exertion which might be necessary to ascertain the exact effect of the water supply on the progress of the epidemic," he wrote in 1855, shortly after the infections dissipated or disappeared.[3]

The experiment Snow devised was, as he described it, "on the grandest scale," with "no fewer than three hundred thousand people of both sexes, of every age and occupation, and of every rank and station, from gentlefolk down to the very poor, divided into two groups without their choice, and, in most cases, without their knowledge; one group being supplied with water containing the sewage of London, and, amongst it, whatever might have come from the cholera patients, the other group having water quite free from such impurity."

At the experiment's end, the mapping results showed that the people who risked infection were those who had drunk the river-contaminated water. To further augment his theory that water contaminated with feces was the causative agent, he described the now famous Broad Street pump episode where cholera infected individuals had drawn water from the well at the Broad Street pump in Soho.

"The most terrible outbreak of cholera which ever occurred in this kingdom," Snow wrote in 1854,

> is probably that which took place in (Soho's) Broad Street, Golden Square, and the adjoining streets, a few weeks ago. Within two hundred and fifty yards of the spot where Cambridge Street joins Broad Street, there were upwards of five hundred fatal attacks of cholera in ten days. The mortality in this limited area probably equals any that was ever caused in this country, even by the plague; and it was much more sudden, as the greater number of cases terminated in a few hours. The mortality would undoubtedly have been much greater had it not been for the flight of the population.

The tale of the Broad Street pump's role in the cholera epidemic of 1854 is known to every student of epidemiology, and it presents a forceful illustration of the importance of homework. Here's an excerpt from Snow's account of the pump's role in spreading the contagion:

> I found that nearly all the deaths had taken place within a short distance of the pump. ... The result of the inquiry then was that there had been no particular outbreak or increase of cholera in this part of London except among the persons who were in the habit of drinking the water of the above-mentioned pump-well. ... The sewer, which passes within a few yards of the well, is twenty-two feet below the surface. Mr. Eley, the percussion-cap manufacturer of 37 Broad Street, informed me that he had long noticed that the water became offensive, both to the smell and taste, after it had been kept about two days. ... I had an interview with the Board of Guardians of St. James's parish, on the evening of Thursday, 7th September, and represented the above circumstances to them. In consequence of what I said, the handle of the pump was removed on the following day— effectively disabling the deadly well.[4]

Removing the pump handle and drawing purer water from a clean well proved effective in eliminating cholera infections in the Broad Street neighborhood. The common contaminant of both the Thames water and the well water tainted by a leaking sewer pipe was feces.

Excerpts from Snow's classic article about cholera clearly demonstrate his powers of observation and reasoning:

> The soiled bed linen and body linen of the patient should be immersed in water as soon as they are removed, until such time as they can be washed, lest the evacuations should become dry, and be wafted about as a fine dust. Articles of bedding and clothing which cannot be washed should be exposed for some time to a temperature of 212 degrees or upwards. Care should be taken that the water employed for drinking and preparing food (whether it come from a pump-well, or be conveyed in pipes) is not contaminated with the contents of cesspools, house-drains, or sewers; or, in the event that water free from suspicion cannot be obtained, is should be well boiled, and, if possible, also filtered.[5]

He also spoke of hand washing and additional precautions, in the same article, to protect against cholera transmission, all of which are still good advice for preventing infectious diseases, even in the twenty-first century. This advice may be even more important now because of the availability of medical methods to reduce stomach acid. Stomach acid kills the organisms of cholera. Individuals who have reduced stomach acid from an operation or are on proton pump inhibitors or antacids to reduce stomach acid are more at risk if they ingest the germ.

Despite Snow's having used valid procedures and solid scientific method in his experiment, both his fellow physicians and the country's scientific community defied him, clinging to the prevailing wisdom that cholera was caused by vaguely defined elements in the atmosphere.

The Lancet, England's (and arguably the world's) leading medical journal, led the assault with an editorial in its June 23, 1855, issue.

"Dr. Snow claims to have discovered that the law of propagation of cholera is the drinking of sewage water," the editorial stated. "His theory, of course, displaces all other theories. Other theories attribute great efficacy in the spread of cholera to bad drainage and atmospheric impurities. Therefore, says Dr. Snow, gases from animal and vegetable decompositions are innocuous! If this logic does not satisfy reason, it satisfies a theory; and we all know that theory is often more despotic than reason. The fact is, that the well whence Dr. Snow draws all sanitary truth is the main sewer. His ... den is a drain. In riding his hobby very hard, he has fallen down through a gully-hole and has never since been able to get out again. And to Dr. Snow an impossible one: so there we leave him."[6]

It wasn't until Robert Koch in 1884 described *Vibrio cholerae* as the cause of cholera that it was accepted as the scientific etiology. But the first to identify the bacillus and document it as the causative agent in a published medical paper was Filippo Pacini in 1854, an Italian anatomist who pinpointed the bacteria by dissecting cholera victims' intestines and microscopically demonstrating the presence of the *Vibrio bacillus*. At the time, the scientific community ignored his findings.[7]

The cases of Snow and Pacini show that doing one's homework and making a monumental discovery does not guarantee that the new information will be accepted. This has been the history of many innovative leaders.

Snow died of a stroke at age forty-five, in 1858, less than three years after publishing his findings. His life was short by modern longevity standards, but his impact on the world of medicine was immense. Some have cited him as the most important physician in history because his work gave birth to the science of epidemiology.

He is buried in London's Brompton Cemetery. The monument marking his grave was destroyed during a World War II bombing raid, but was later restored.[8]

•   •   •

Snow's pioneering work shows the importance of homework. One can extrapolate that lesson to any challenge. It doesn't matter if you are doing public health in a distant land or caring for the injured in a war zone. Leaders do their homework and anticipate what could happen to their colleagues working in the field or in a war zone. They prepare by consulting or having available a physician who has anticipated what could happen and can advise about how to handle the problem.

Doing our homework applies in all areas of our lives. At a meeting, when a debate arises from a proposal, it is important to have two copies of the proposal on hand when you present your case—one to quote from if anyone challenges you on the accuracy of your remarks, the other for the moderator or person conducting the meeting to verify your statements should you be challenged. This prevents someone from saying, "There appears to be confusion as to what the bill actually says, so let's table the issue until the next meeting."

Doing homework also is called for when awaiting a job interview. An applicant is more likely to be hired if he or she did proper research. Advance preparation can make it obvious that you understand the job, you are knowledgeable about the company, and that you clearly have the skills needed. Anticipating questions beforehand gives you time to reflect and give concise, impressive answers.

Be prepared by anticipating such questions as:

- What is your strongest quality for this job? What is your weakest?

- Tell me the greatest job mistake you ever made and how you handled it. What did you learn from it?
- What should I have asked you in this interview that I failed to ask?

The message of doing one's homework has been repeated through the centuries. Over 2,500 years ago, Sun Tzu instructed in *The Art of War*, "Know the enemy and know yourself; in a hundred battles you will never be in peril."

During World War II Patton routinely studied his adversaries and their tactics. A Patton diary entry reads: "Woke up at 0300 and it was raining like hell. I actually got nervous and got up and read Rommel's book, *Infantry Attacks*. It was most helpful, as he described all the rains he had in September, 1914, and also the fact that, in spite of the heavy rains, the Germans got along."[9]

Studying history and the maneuvers of past wars also benefited Patton's contemporary, MacArthur. U.S. Representative Isaac Newton Skelton, a student of U.S. military history, cites MacArthur's reliance on the study of history in formulating military strategy and tactics. Skelton provides this example:

[MacArthur's] September 15, 1950, landing at Inchon—deep behind North Korean lines, culminating in a hammer-and-anvil decimation of Communist forces between Seoul and Pusan—stands as one of the most brilliant and daring operations in the annals of warfare. MacArthur had first-hand combat experience to draw from in crafting the Inchon-Seoul campaign. He had orchestrated eighty-seven amphibious assaults in the Pacific campaign against the Japanese during World War II. MacArthur, however, also drew from history. As Army Chief of Staff in 1935, he advised that the military student "extend his analytic interest to the dust-buried accounts of wars long past as well as those still reeking with the scent of battle" to "bring to light those fundamental principles, and their combinations and applications which, in the past, have been productive of success." MacArthur operationalized the words of Karl von Clausewitz, written 118 years earlier: "A swift and vigorous transition to attack—the flashing sword of vengeance—is the most brilliant point of the defensive."[10]

Two obvious questions are: How does one do the homework? Where does one gather the information?

I vividly remember what my professor of surgery, Dr. Oscar Creech of the Tulane University School of Medicine, said in the 1960s: "After two nights in the medical library you will know more than ninety percent of people in the world on a given topic. Of course, you will not have the experience, but you'll find out all there is to know before asking questions. Ask questions about the truly unknown."

Two nights in the library meant going to *Index Medicus*, a listing of articles, and then checking to see if the library had the articles readily available. Today we have the Internet, which travels at the speed of light to the greatest libraries in the world.

The Web

The Web is a good source to start searching for information. Although a lot of it can be unreliable, one can make an effort to visit trustworthy sources to reduce the risk of ending up with opinions unsupported by facts.

Let's do a sample search. Suppose you're a medical student or physician who wants information about treatment of breast cancer. You go to a search engine and look for official sites of well known medical centers or schools. You also can go directly to the National Library of Medicine and use PubMed, a search engine designed for easy use by both physicians and nonphysicians. PubMed will yield citations of scientific articles, many with summaries.[11]

Of course, the Web is the greatest library ever assembled, and the yield of citations through a search engine can be huge. There are many search engines. Among the better known are Google.com, Yahoo. com, Ask Jeeves (Ask.com), and WebCrawler.com. The University of California at Berkeley recommends the first three.

The Berkeley Web site[12] includes a page on "Teaching Library Internet Workshops," which contends that "Google alone is often not sufficient," and that "Less than half the searchable Web is fully searchable in Google. Overlap studies show that about half of the pages in any search engine database exist only in that database. Getting a second opinion is therefore often worth your time."[13]

The Web site explains which search engines use full Boolean logic (an algebraic system of logical operations) and which ones use only part of it. Among the advantages of Boolean logic is that it speeds up the search and excludes items you do not wish to have returned in the search yield. For example, the Yahoo search engine supports full Boolean logic. The UC Berkeley page states that Yahoo "Accepts AND, OR, NOT or ( ). You must enclose terms joined by OR in parentheses (classic Boolean)." Google.com and Ask.com only have partial Boolean logic.

Sometimes one Web site is all you need, and trusted sites may be found quickly even with an enormous number of links reported. Using "breast cancer treatment" as the Google search term, more than twenty-five million links were found, an overwhelming number. But the third link listed was the National Cancer Institute, a source of information reviewed by experts. One of the links at the institute's site is "treatment option." The link mentions four types of standard treatment: surgery, radiation therapy, chemotherapy, and hormone therapy. Some of these treatments may be combined, depending on the clinical stage of the disease.[14]

The fifth link among the twenty-five million sites reported by Google is the Web site of the Mayo Clinic. The link takes you to a page outlining the various therapies, including the different types of surgery available.[15]

Search engines also can be capable of finding more than text, such as photos of the person you are trying to gather information about, or recent news articles about the person.

Books

Textbooks and research papers are other good sources of information; but it's useful to remember that, with today's exponential growth of knowledge, books can quickly become out of date. However, a public library is a good place to start, and the research librarian there can help supplement the books with periodicals or can suggest specific Web searches.

Consultants

Locate a specialist in the category of information you need. If you're a physician or medical student with a question about the kidneys, talk to a urologist or a nephrologist. Information about flying is best acquired from a pilot. If you need to know what it means to be in a prisoner of war camp, talk to someone who spent time in one.

Experts help to separate factual and important information from rumor or misinformation. If you want to know what it is like to be in a shooting war, talk to someone who served on the front lines or behind enemy lines as a scout, and not an armchair general or someone who has never been in the military.

The point here is to go to primary sources rather than secondary ones. Then, when you're continuing to develop leadership skills, you'll have the best available information.

Reliable Sources

Trust must be earned, and a leader learns through time and experience which sources can be trusted for reliable information, allowing quicker action. A reliable source provides objective facts—no hyperbole, no embellishment.

A leader also researches and tests any necessary equipment before using it. If a potential problem exists with the equipment, it should be found and resolved through testing. The situation may not be a matter of life or death in a surgical procedure. It may be a matter of taking a photo that has the potential for a Pulitzer Prize, or closing a multimillion-dollar deal.

Once information is obtained from research, it is often helpful to have the data reviewed by an expert who can validate it and put it into perspective. Using this option has considerable importance in medical research.

Amateurs don't test, they don't prepare. Leaders try not to leave anything to chance.

Shortcuts to Data Retrieval

Encyclopedias once were the gold standard for learning about a subject. But with today's technology and exponential growth of knowledge, a printed encyclopedia is almost out of date the moment it arrives at the bookstore.

The obvious alternative is to turn to the Internet. Most Web sites are regularly updated, although the information in some seemingly authoritative Web sites can be questioned. One such source is Wikipedia, an open-access encyclopedia site whose information can be edited by virtually any user. When using sites like this one, the listed references should be checked to determine if the information came from a peer-reviewed source.

The new mobility of computers has dramatically increased their usefulness. One truly helpful device is the personal digital assistant (PDA), a portable, handheld computer that performs a wide range of functions. Many have Internet access built into the device. Wireless cards also can provide PDAs or larger notebook computers with an Internet connection, allowing them to download information that can be retrieved later with a keyword search. Some search engines treat every word as a keyword, making a PDA an invaluable tool during discussions at meetings, when relevant documents stored in computer files can be accessed, often in a matter of seconds.

I once served on an advisory committee looking into health-system reform. At one important committee meeting, the discussion focused on methods of tracking infections that occurred in the hospitals of a certain state. While one presenter was stating his case, he mentioned a certain Web site that was especially relevant. This allowed me to use my notebook computer, equipped with the necessary wireless card, to access the site. I also could have used my BlackBerry phone/PDA for the same search but it is a little more cumbersome to search compared to the notebook computer.

From the search I learned that at least eight of the hospitals had reported no infections. That a hospital could experience zero infections was astounding to me. Either the reports were not accurate or the hospitals had developed a superior method of infection prevention. If the former was true, the data was worthless. If the latter was true, I thought we should all learn the technique so it could be used worldwide.

I asked the presenter if all hospital records regarding infections were inspected on-site, lessening the potential for wrong statistics. He said they were not. The committee's chairperson asked if I was satisfied with the answer. I said that I was not, although I considered the testimony enlightening. I told the committee that, based on the faulty method used to collect the information, I certainly would not send this data to the *Journal of the American Medical Association* or the *New England Journal of Medicine* and expect the expert reviewers to recommend publication.

This anecdote shows the power of doing the homework by accessing information quickly and exposing data that was based on faulty methods.

Rules of the Game

A leader does not leave anything to chance. In any endeavor, it is important to know the rules of the game. If a meeting room is the battleground, one should know parliamentary procedure. Someone who'll be testifying before a governmental committee must research the topic well, anticipate the questions and be ready to testify for a period as brief as five minutes and as long as four hours, depending on the topic and how controversial it is.

I've had the experience of having to answer questions for four hours, and I learned that this is one method governmental officials use to determine if you really know the subject or if you're a token speaker reading someone else's written position.

Lessons Learned

- Homework is a necessary preparation for success and leadership. Use a variety of sources (starting with the Internet) to do as much homework as possible.
- Observation and logical pursuit of the evidence lead to the truth.
- Innovators frequently are in the minority and have to fight to get the truth recognized.
- The pursuit of excellence and leadership can be a lonely path, but success is worth the potholes encountered en route.

CHAPTER 5

COURAGE

Whereas, Sir, you know courage is reckoned the
greatest of all virtues; because, unless a man has that
virtue, he has no security for preserving any other.

—Samuel Johnson, quoted in James Boswell's
Life of Johnson, 1791

The presidential race was the news of the day. After
a dinner, a candidate stood up, waving his hat in
answer to the cheers of the crowd. He was headed to
the auditorium for his speech. Suddenly, a small man
pushed his way through the crowd to within a few feet
of the candidate and fired a gun at his heart. The bullet entered the left chest. Another man leaped on the
shooter and wrestled him to the ground with a choke-
hold around the assassin's throat, disarming him.

A thick manuscript was in the left side of the candidate's coat and reduced the force of the bullet, but
the bullet entered his chest. The candidate insisted

on going to the auditorium to deliver his speech. He moved his eyes across the large audience. After a dramatic pause, he began speaking without notes. He said, in part;

> Friends, I shall ask you to be as quiet as possible. I don't know whether you fully understand that I have just been shot; but it takes more than that to kill a Bull Moose. But fortunately I had my manuscript, so you see I was going to make a long speech, and there is a bullet—there is where the bullet went through—and it probably saved me from it going into my heart. The bullet is in me now, so that I cannot make a very long speech, but I will try my best.
>
> And now, friends, I want to take advantage of this incident to say a word of solemn warning to my fellow countrymen. First of all, I want to say this about myself: I have altogether too important things to think of to feel any concern over my own death; and now I cannot speak to you insincerely within five minutes of being shot. ... I can tell you with absolute truthfulness that I am very much uninterested in whether I am shot or not. It was just as when I was colonel of my regiment. I always felt that a private was to be excused for feeling at times some pangs of anxiety about his personal safety, but I cannot understand a man fit to be a colonel who can pay any heed to his personal safety when he is occupied as he ought to be with the absorbing desire to do his duty.

At one time I promoted five men for gallantry on the field of battle. Afterward in making some inquiries about them I found that two of them were Protestants, two Catholic and one a Jew. One Protestant came from Germany and one was born in Ireland. I did not promote them because of their religion. It just happened that way. If all five of them had been Jews I would have promoted them, or if all five of them had been Protestants I would have promoted them; or if they had been Catholics. In that regiment I had a man born in Italy who distinguished himself by gallantry; there was another young fellow, a son of Polish parents, and another who came here when he was a child from Bohemia, who likewise distinguished themselves; and friends, I assure you, that I was incapable of considering any question whatever, but the worth of each individual as a fighting man. If he was a good fighting man, then I saw that Uncle Sam got the benefit of it. That is all.[1]

As the *Detroit Free Press* reported on October 15, 1912, President Theodore Roosevelt "delivered part of his scheduled address with the bullet in his body, his blood staining his white vest as he spoke to a huge throng at the auditorium. Later, he collapsed, weakened by the wound, and was rushed to Emergency hospital."[2]

Many are familiar with the most famous part of Roosevelt's "The Man in the Arena" speech, given in 1910 at the Sorbonne in Paris, about the critic not counting:

> It is not the critic who counts, not the man who points out how the strong man stumbled, or where the doer of deeds could have done better. The credit belongs to the man who is actually in the arena, whose face is marred by dust and sweat and blood, who strives valiantly, who errs and comes short again and again, who knows the great enthusiasms, the great devotions, and spends himself in a worthy cause, who at best knows achievement and who at the worst if he fails at least fails while daring greatly so that his place shall never be with those cold and timid souls who know neither victory nor defeat.[3]

Roosevelt, leader of the Rough Riders and a conservationist noted for his establishment of many national parks, was a fearless man. His courage has been celebrated in history. His image is among those of Washington, Jefferson, and Lincoln carved on Mount Rushmore in South Dakota. He is the only president to have received both the Congressional Medal of Honor and the Nobel Peace Prize.

An English statesman, Viscount Lee of Fareham, said this about him: "Of all the public men that I have known, on both sides of the Atlantic (and there are few that I have not known in the past thirty years), he stands out the greatest, and as the most potent influence for good upon the life of his generation."[4]

Others agree with the quotation at the start of this chapter about the importance of courage. Robert Kennedy wrote of his brother President John F. Kennedy: "Courage is the virtue that President Kennedy most admired. He sought out those people who had demonstrated in some way, whether it was on a battlefield or a baseball diamond, in a speech or fighting for a cause, that they had courage, that they would stand up, that they could be counted on."[5]

John Kennedy himself said this about courage in his Pulitzer Prize–winning book *Profiles in Courage*, written when he was a freshman senator: "In whatever area in life one may meet the challenges of courage, whatever may be the sacrifices he faces if he follows his conscience—the loss of his friends, his fortune, his contentment, even the esteem of his fellow men—each man must decide for himself the course he will follow. The stories of past courage can define that ingredient—they can teach, they can offer hope, they can provide inspiration. But they cannot supply courage itself. For this each man must look into his own soul."[6]

Some will try to thwart potential leaders who want to move forward courageously by saying the challenge is impossible. Those who are challenged by naysayers might do well to remember the example of a nineteenth-century Hungarian obstetrician,

Ignaz Semmelweis, whose studies led to the use of antiseptics, first in obstetrics and later in other medical fields. Joseph Lister, a pioneer in sterile surgery, was influenced by his work and Semmelweis is now seen as a trailblazer in the use of antiseptics.

While teaching in a Vienna hospital during the 1840s, Semmelweis and his colleagues were puzzled by the high frequency of fatal puerperal fever ("childbirth fever") infections occurring in women during childbirth. The number of infections was higher for hospital births than for deliveries on the streets.

Semmelweis conducted an experiment tracking the practices of midwives, medical students, and physicians, and learned that medical students and physicians in obstetrics wards were treating women in labor without having first washed their hands after leaving the autopsy room. A physician friend of Semmelweis cut himself with the scalpel during an autopsy and died of sepsis. An autopsy showed that the friend's organs showed infection similar to the women who died of puerperal fever. He then made the connection of contamination between the autopsy room and sepsis.

The midwives did not work in the autopsy room. Patients delivered by medical students had a puerperal fever incidence rate of eighteen percent whereas those delivered by the midwives had a rate of two percent.

Semmelweis directed all students to scrub their hands with chlorine before obstetric examinations, and the hospital's death rate from the deadly fever fell drastically, equaling the level of the midwives. However, physicians in Vienna did not accept his documentation, and he subsequently moved to Hungary's Pest Hospital, where he enforced a rule of strict antiseptic techniques and reduced the puerperal fever death rate to less than one percent. Yet, once again, hospital authorities resisted using his techniques.[7]

Why do naysayers exist? Sometimes it is jealousy. Sometimes it is a reluctance to give up the ways that the naysayers are expert in. When a paradigm shift takes place, everybody is at the starting line. The expertise in the discarded method is now of no value. The inability to take responsibility for a bad practice or the feeling of guilt for causing the deaths of patients may be an important subconscious motivation in some instances.

An example of the latter is the tragic story of Gustav Adolf Michaelis, an obstetrician in Kiel, Germany. He confirmed Semmelweis's theory and began to practice it. But the weight of the knowledge that his previous practices had caused the death of many of his patients, including that of his niece, depressed him greatly and he committed suicide by throwing himself under a train.[8]

Yes, you will meet critics. And you will encounter circumstances that may make you fearful. Such is life.

Congressional Medal of Honor winner, Nick Bacon of Arkansas, said, "No one is exempt from fear." And another winner, John Hawk of California, now living in Washington State, said, "Courage is not a lack of fear—which would be a lack of intelligence—but it is how you handle your fear."[9]

You can overcome the fear and embrace courage. They certainly did.

Remember, Theodore Roosevelt said that it was not the critic who counts; it is the man in the arena. And the same can be said about those who try to intimidate or blame you. They don't count when you pursue the right thing or stand up against injustice. It requires courage to stay in the arena, but the long-term rewards outweigh the illusion of temporary safety. As Kipling said in "If":

> *If you can keep your head when all about you*
> *Are losing theirs and blaming it on you;*
> *If you can trust yourself when all men doubt you,*
> *But make allowance for their doubting too; ...*
> *Yours is the Earth and everything that's in it,*
> *And—which is more—you'll be a Man my son!*

Without courage, the best plans fail. Courage is the fuel of accomplishment. It's crucial to observe and study to gain knowledge, to experience new adventures, to reflect and gain insight, to reach wisdom. But courage is needed for action. Knowing what to do without action is akin to Brownian motion, purposeless shaking in the same location. It is not leadership. Leadership is movement toward the goal. As Ernest Hemingway said, "Never mistake motion for action."

Courage allows us to take action. Leonardo da Vinci, a true leader and polymath, said, "I have been impressed with the urgency of doing. Knowing is not enough; we must apply. Being willing is not enough; we must do."[10]

In 2001 I nominated the Bill and Melinda Gates Foundation for the American Medical Association's Dr. Nathan Davis International Award in Medicine and Public Health for Outstanding Global Health Initiative, which they received. The Gates have focused worldwide on children's health, vaccine development, and disease eradication. I argued that their foundation raised the international betterment of public health to a level never before attained. Consider that every physician draws strength from the saving of a life. Such wonderful one-on-one efforts are multiplied a million-fold by the Gates Foundation's programs.[11]

Their foundation has contributed more than the Carnegie foundations and the Rockefeller and Ford foundations combined, even when the donations of all four philanthropies are converted to present dollar values. The Gates Foundation awards total $1 billion annually, and much of this money goes to the Global Health Program to eliminate dreaded diseases. The range of the activities is on a scale never before seen in the history of philanthropy.

Once, over a cup of coffee, I asked Melinda French Gates to think about the definition of leadership and send me her thoughts. She said,

> The person who embodies leadership for me is Nelson Mandela. Mandela inspired the world with his strength and courage in leading the fight against apartheid. His commitment to the goal of a democratic and free South Africa, where everyone—regardless of skin color—shares an opportunity and a stake in the country's future, never wavered. Many great leaders show courage, but Mandela, who was imprisoned for 27 years, coupled that courage with compassion and the ability to forgive. South Africa might not have made a successful transition without Mandela's leadership and grace.[12]

Ernest Hemingway would no doubt agree, as he said, "Courage is grace under pressure."[13]

Significant events in history have always coupled leadership with courage. Courage was necessary for the birth of the United States of America, a country that remains a land of liberty and freedom because of courage. As Medal of Honor winner Lewis Millett said, "We are a free country. Why are we? Because a lot of people—black, white, yellow—gave their lives so that you and I could live free. Simple as that."[14]

Opportunities for demonstrating courage exist in everyone's life. To be courageous, one doesn't have to lead the charge up a hill against the enemy in war with bullets flying, or fight against discrimination and remain in prison for refusing to bow to apartheid. The option of standing up for what is right, regardless of the personal consequences, is available to each of us. A supposed leader is a sham without courage.

Lessons Learned

- Courage is the fuel for leadership. There is no leadership without courage.
- Courage is not the absence of fear. Courage is acting in spite of fear.
- Naysayers and excuses for reasons not to act abound. Ignore them.
- Action is an essential ingredient for leadership, and courage starts the journey.
- Each of us has the opportunity to be courageous.

CHAPTER 6

PERSISTENCE: "DON'T GIVE UP!"

Nothing in the world can take the place of persistence. Talent will not; nothing is more common than unsuccessful men with talent. Genius will not; unrewarded genius is almost a proverb. Education will not; the world is full of educated derelicts. Persistence and determination are omnipotent. The slogan "press on" has solved and always will solve the problems of the human race.

—Calvin Coolidge[1]

By 1961, the United States and the Soviet Union had been engaged for years in the game of brinkmanship known as the Cold War. Four years previously, the Soviets had launched the first satellite into outer space.

On May 25, 1961, John F. Kennedy, the president
of the United States, stood before a joint session of
Congress and delivered a special message on urgent
national needs. After defining the country's role in
the defense of freedom, he said:

> I believe that this nation should commit itself to
> achieving the goal, before this decade is out, of land-
> ing a man on the moon and returning him safely to
> the earth. No single space project in this period will
> be more impressive to mankind, or more important
> for the long-range exploration of space. ... If we are
> to go only half way, or reduce our sights in the face
> of difficulty, in my judgment it would be better not
> to go at all.[2]

One critical issue was whether the U.S. could
develop and test a larger rocket to get a man to the
moon and return him safely. One Langley Research
Center engineer, John Houbolt, theorized some
months before that there was an advantage in accomplishing a moon landing using a multiple stage flight
with the parent craft orbiting around the moon before
a landing craft descended to the moon surface. This
was called lunar orbit rendezvous (LOR). This sim-
plification of the flight was akin to an epiphany. He
later described it in a history of NASA by James R.
Hansen, *Enchanted Rendezvous*.[3] Houbolt said that
"almost simultaneously, it became clear that Lunar

Orbit Rendezvous offered a chain reaction simpli-
fication on all 'back effects': development, testing,
manufacturing, erection, countdown, flight operations, et cetera. It 'clicked'—'all would be simplified.'
This is fantastic. If there is any idea we have to push,
it is this one! I vowed to dedicate myself to the task."
Thus there would not be a need to develop an unusually large rocket. The payload could be reduced dramatically.

The LOR concept would use four components: the
proven Saturn V rocket for liftoff and three distinct
"modules" to perform other functions.[4] The command
module would contain the crew and controls. The service module's purposes would be propulsion and support. The lunar module, named "Eagle," would be the
only craft to touch down on the moon's surface. After
the Saturn V rocket finished its job, the command
and service modules and Eagle would orbit the moon.
Eagle then would detach and descend to the moon's
surface with the astronauts inside. When Eagle later
departed the Moon, it would rejoin the command and
service modules and the astronauts would transfer
into the command module and later jettison the lunar
craft Eagle on the return journey to Earth.

Just before entering Earth's atmosphere, the service module would be detached, with only the command module returning to Earth in the splashdown.

Once Houbolt realized his concept of LOR,
which was finally accepted by NASA for Project

Apollo in July 1962, he "proved to be NASA's most dedicated, active, eloquent, stubborn, and informed crusader for what came to he known as 'the LOR concept.'"[5]

But there was strong opposition to his idea. At a NASA briefing where both the administrator and Wernher von Braun were present, Houbolt concluded with enthusiasm that the weight savings for the liftoff would be two to two and a half times less. "When he finished, his long-time Langley associate [said] 'His figures lie, he doesn't know what he's talking about.'

"Houbolt tried to stay calm, but clearly he was agitated. He answered the charge [with] he 'ought to look at the study before [making] a pronouncement like that.' It was an 'ought to' that Houbolt would be passing on to many other LOR skeptics before it was all over.

"But if a rendezvous around the moon failed, the astronauts would be too far away to be saved, because nothing could be done. The morbid specter of dead astronauts sailing around the moon haunted the dreams of those responsible for the Apollo program. It was a nightmare that made objective evaluation of the LOR concept by NASA unusually difficult."[6]

The opponents favored a direct ascent or an Earth-orbit rendezvous.

According to NASA, "the LOR concept was a 'long shot'—almost not worthy of mention for many NASA officials."

The director of the Office of Space Flight Programs at NASA headquarters came in to address the members. He said, "Well, look fellas, I want you to understand something. I've been right most of my life about things, and if you guys are going to talk about rendezvous, any kind of rendezvous, as a way of going to the Moon, forget it. I've heard all those schemes and I don't want to hear any more of them, because we're not going to the Moon using any of those schemes."[7]

Houbolt did not give up. He sent a letter to the second in command at NASA on November 15, 1961, skipping his structured chain of command.

"Do we want to go to the moon or not?" Houbolt wrote. "And if so, why do we have to restrict our thinking to a certain narrow channel?" Using this reasoning, Houbolt questioned the acceptance of a larger, untested rocket. "Why is Nova, with its ponderous size simply just accepted, and why is a much less grandiose scheme involving rendezvous ostracized or put on the defensive?"

In the end, despite all the opposition, critical analysis of the facts convinced NASA that Houbolt was correct. When the official announcement was made about LOR, his division chief informed him by saying, "Congratulations, John. They've adopted your scheme. I can safely say I'm shaking hands with the man who single-handedly saved the government $20 billion."

Houbolt won a special award from NASA in 1963 for his work on LOR. It said in part: "For his foresight, perseverance, and incisive theoretical analysis."

"Six years later, at 4:17 p.m. (Eastern Daylight Time) on July 20th, 1969, John Houbolt, by then a senior consultant with the innovative Aeronautical Research Associates of Princeton, New Jersey, sat inconspicuously as one of the 'nest' of invited guests and dignitaries in the viewing room of Mission Control at the Manned Spacecraft Center in Houston. Like so many others around the world at that moment, he listened in wonder to the deliberately spoken, yet wildly dramatic words of Neil A. Armstrong: 'Houston, Tranquility Base here. The Eagle has landed.'" At that moment, "[t]urning from his seat, NASA's master rocketeer, Wernher von Braun, found Houbolt's eye among all the others, gave him the okay sign, and said to him simply, 'John, it worked beautifully.'"[8]

Shortly after, Neil Armstrong walked on the Moon and said: "That's one small step for a man, one giant leap for mankind."[9] Here were Americans walking on the moon, the first in the history of the world.

"Houbolt" was speechless at what would be the greatest moment in his professional life—not to mention one of the greatest moments in human existence. But this crusader was thinking, "By golly, the world ought to stop right at this moment."[10]

• • •

Houbolt's is a dramatic story of a man who passionately pursued his idea despite great pressure to conform to the majority opinion. As Aldous Huxley said about such situations, "Facts don't cease to exist because they are ignored." But others can make the wrong choice if a leader doesn't come forth and courageously persist with the facts.

As NASA noted when quoting the 1982 view of George Low, a space pioneer and engineer, "It is my opinion to this day that had the Lunar Orbit Rendezvous Mode not been chosen, Apollo would not have succeeded."

Persistence is necessary for success in any field of endeavor and is an essential ingredient of leadership. The National Federation of Independent Business calls persistence the essence of success. As with adverse winds when sailing, some curse the winds; leaders learn to tack by moving the bow and sail and continue to move toward their destination.

Leadership is refusing to accept the first failure as the end of a journey. The journey could be as simple as trying to reach someone by phone. If the response is "Not in," try to locate the person. Find a way to get around a blocking secretary or "gatekeeper." Page the individual if there is a paging system or use another means such as e-mail. Be creative in the pursuit.

Persistence can produce great rewards. Once, when I was in the military and far from New Orleans, I needed expert advice regarding a patient who was near death. I was able to reach the famous surgeon Dr. Alton Ochsner, Sr., at Ochsner Foundation Hospital, by having him paged. The hospital telephone operator told me Dr. Ochsner had left for South America. I asked that he be paged anyway and I reached him minutes before he departed the building for the airport. He answered the page immediately, and gave me good advice. "Hang up the phone and operate immediately," he said. Without delay I performed the procedure he recommended and saved a woman's life.

Persistence does not mean one performs the exact same action and expects success. If an impediment exists in the procedure or plan, persistence with that error does not advance you on the path to leadership. Do not persist in error. One should analyze failure by examining the steps that led to it. By analysis, one can change systems and reduce the risk of error or failure. Simply telling people not to let an error occur again does not guarantee its prevention regardless of their best intentions. Error is an unintentional act. The best way to prevent the error is not by admonition but by changing the system so that it becomes impossible for the error to reoccur.

An example in medicine is the risk of pumping air into a patient's blood stream. Years ago this could happen when a patient was in shock from blood loss. "Pump the blood in!" was the cry from the chief surgeon. Rapid infusion of blood was essential to keep the patient alive. The procedure was to force blood into the patient from a glass bottle of donor blood by pumping air into the bottle. The danger was that, if the person infusing the blood was distracted by another crisis, all of the blood could empty from the glass bottle, and air would go to the patient's heart, causing death. The system fix was to replace the glass bottle with a collapsible plastic blood container. A pressure cuff was placed completely around the plastic bag and then the pressure cuff was pumped up. This compressed the plastic blood container and blood went into the patient under pressure. When the blood bag was emptied completely, there was no risk of air entering the patient.

As Ross Perot, one of America's most successful businessmen, once said, "Most people give up just when they're about to achieve success. They give up at the last minute of the game, one foot from a winning touchdown." And of course, who cannot comprehend the power of Winston Churchill's persistence when faced with the onslaught of Nazi Germany and the bombing of London in World War II. At that time, he said, "Never give in—never, never, never, never, in nothing great or small, large or petty, never give in except to convictions of honor and good sense. Never yield to force; never yield to the apparently overwhelming might of the enemy."

Churchill's words come to mind when I recall the time I was helping another surgeon operate on a young man injured in an auto accident. The injured man was about twenty-three years old and was bleeding inside his abdomen. We managed to stop the bleeding, but, as we were ending the operation and, despite restoring the lost blood and the anesthesiologist giving oxygen via the endotracheal tube, the patient's heart stopped beating. External cardiac compression was done, but it did not restore the heartbeat. The anesthesiologist shook his head and said, "There is nothing more we can do. We must pronounce him dead."

At that moment, I refused to believe that this young man was dead. Everything that was supposed to be done was done. I pulled back the drapes covering the patient's chest, splashed antiseptic on his chest and cut it open. I reached for his lifeless heart and began to squeeze it between my hands. I told the anesthesiologist to keep squeezing the breathing bag filled with oxygen. I could not leave that room without saying to myself that EVERYTHING possible had been done. Suddenly, between squeezes on the heart, I felt it start beating!

That young man recovered, became a talented engineer, and accomplished great engineering feats all over the world. He frequently sent postcards from exotic places to the surgeon I assisted and thanked the surgeon for keeping him alive.

Dramatic events like this one may be rare, but I've experienced countless joys during the normal course of the noble profession of medicine and watched others refuse to give up when seeking some new scientific discovery. I tell medical students that this approach will stay in their consciousness and instill a sense of joy in them when temporary obstacles threaten to overwhelm them. They will have similar stories and they will rejoice that they are healers.

Each of us can craft our own destiny regardless of our vocation. But doing so demands persistence.

Lessons Learned

- Genius and talent amount to naught if one doesn't persist in pursuit of the goal.
- Persistence doesn't mean blind repetition when failure occurs. It does mean analysis to see if the conclusion or approach is correct and if so, pursuing that approach. If changes need to be made, do so, and continue on.
- Draw encouragement from stories that show how persistence leads to success. Search for more stories. Every such story contains a lesson for those whose minds remain open to new ideas.

CHAPTER 7

DECISIVENESS

The person who in shaky times also wavers only increases the evil, but the person of firm decision fashions the universe.

—Johann Wolfgang Von Goethe

It was Friday, April 3, 1970, a clear and visibility-unrestricted day—or "CAVU" in pilots' lingo—when the phone rang. The caller was my chief master sergeant: "A B-52 just crashed on landing!" he said. "I'll pick you up in the Jeep. I have the operating instruments that you'll need. The plane is aflame and the navigator is trapped by the navigation panel crushing his leg. You'll have to amputate."

As we approached the Stratofortress bomber, black smoke loomed ominously above the giant aircraft, one of those most feared by America's enemies, and capable of carrying nuclear bombs or massive amounts of conventional explosives. Here was the plane that was dramatically portrayed in the movie *Dr. Strangelove* and now was melting like a plastic model in the intense heat.

Would any of the crew survive this hellish tragedy? As we drew near the plane we received word that all but two of the crew had been removed alive from the inferno. Still alive, but trapped in the smoke-filled plane, was the navigator, held by his large, dial-filled navigation panel that was bent grotesquely down against his right knee and lower leg. The tailgunner also was trapped in the bubble turret at the rear of the plane. The flames continued to rush down the fuselage toward him despite the best efforts of the firemen heroically attacking the flames with everything available. Smoke inhalation and exhaustion of oxygen could kill the tailgunner at any moment even if the fire was extinguished. It was then that I witnessed an act of decisiveness and courage that I will remember the rest of my life.

A young airman leaped into the fire truck and slammed the accelerator to the floor. He rammed the truck into the fuselage, and the tailgunner who was trapped in his turret was cut loose from the fuselage and sent tumbling on the runway, where the flames no longer could reach him. Fortunately, he had no significant injuries.

I did not have to enter the plane, as it was possible to use a jack and lift the metal off of the navigator's leg. I operated on his damaged leg and he healed. It was remarkable that no one died as a result of the crash. It was a testimony to the importance of preparation for disasters and teamwork. The Vanderbilt Television News Archive contains the NBC News film showing anchorman Chet Huntley reporting the crash on the day it occurred. The decisiveness of the young airman remains in my memory despite the many years that have passed since his very brave act saved a life.[1]

Decisiveness is democratic and is not limited to rank or stature. This young airman had no high rank but he knew that prompt action was needed to save a life. He made the decision without regard to consequences to himself. That is a critical component of leadership.

• • •

Why do some people have the ability to make quick decisions and perform heroic acts and others procrastinate and get action paralysis?

Fear is the root cause of indecision. The anxiety about making a decision originates from the fear that someone will blame you if the decision does not work out to everyone's satisfaction. Indecision comes from the emotional response to that fear. A true leader looks at the scenario that is unfolding, quickly gathers all available facts, using experts if necessary, and then makes a decision.

In many emergencies, if the person in charge waits until all the relevant facts are gathered before acting, the action could be too late. A victim of an auto accident who is in shock and bleeding from his ruptured spleen needs an immediate operation to stop the bleeding. Waiting for yet another test might provide more information, but the patient could die in the interim.

When lawlessness breaks out after a flood, and people are trapped on rooftops, public officials have to make decisions quickly to save lives and restore order. Arguments about whether one agency or government entity will be in charge, or whether precedents must be followed, is a betrayal of the trust given to elected officials by those whose lives are at risk. As President Theodore Roosevelt once said, "In any moment of decision the best thing you can do is the right thing, the next best thing is the wrong thing, and the worst thing you can do is nothing."

The immediate problem with indecision is the delay. As the nineteenth-century British statesman George Canning said, "Indecision and delays are the parents of failure."[2]

Potential leaders must learn that indecision can lead to a long-term lack of respect and the deaths of others. It is imperative to make a timely decision and move on. There always will be those who, armed with hindsight or bias, are quick to criticize after the fact. The best plan is worthless without the decision to act.

True leaders know the difference between the need for an in-depth study of a problem when there is no immediate crisis, and the need to take control and make emergency decisions when a crisis exists. People want someone in control who can make decisions, communicate candidly about the crisis, keep them informed, and give advice. If an epidemic occurs, the leader assures the public that the best public health official or infectious disease expert from the Centers for Disease Control is present and available to give accurate answers about the spread of the disease and measures to prevent contamination. The true leader doesn't try to answer the scientific questions from the press. Those attempts usually result in errors and an erosion of public trust. People will follow a competent, decisive leader who takes responsibility for decisions and actions taken. An incompetent, indecisive leader loses followers quickly, and chaos develops with a cacophony of voices offering information that may or may not be accurate.

One way to foster decisiveness is to anticipate what could go wrong and determine in advance what you would do. No one has a crystal ball view, but one certainly can prepare "what-if" scenarios in broad categories. Performing a few such exercises will imprint a response pattern that can be activated in a crisis. What if a plane crashed? Would you seize an opportunity to save someone even if your own life was at risk? What if a child ran into the path of an oncoming car? Would you dash from the sidewalk and rush into the street to snatch the child even though the car might hit you? Reflect in advance, decide, and be prepared to act when urgent decision-making becomes necessary.

Lessons Learned

- To be a leader, one must make timely decisions.
- Fear is the root cause of indecision.
- Fear stems from a dread of being blamed if failure ensues.
- Indecision and delays beget failure.
- Learn that the consequences of indecision bring long-term lack of respect and can cause the death of others who depend on the person in authority.
- Make a timely decision and move on. There will always be those who criticize once the results are known. Usually, hindsight bias is their only tool.
- Take responsibility for your decisions and actions.
- Anticipate what could go wrong and be prepared.
- Practice "what-if" scenarios to condition your mind to act in a crisis, even if the crisis puts you at risk.
- The best plan is worthless without the decision to act.

CHAPTER 8

COMMUNICATION

The newest computer can merely compound, at speed, the oldest problem in the relations between human beings, and in the end the communicator will be confronted with the old problem, of what to say and how to say it.[1]

—Edward R. Murrow

It was October 1988 and the two vice presidential candidates, senators Lloyd Bentsen and Dan Quayle, were debating in Omaha, Nebraska. It was dull until Quayle, the young Republican candidate, said, "I have as much experience in the Congress as Jack Kennedy did when he sought the presidency."

Bentsen, the Democratic World War II veteran, responded with a remark that put him in the spotlight and is considered the ultimate putdown:

"Senator," Bentsen said, "I served with Jack Kennedy. I knew Jack Kennedy. Jack Kennedy was a friend of mine. Senator, you're no Jack Kennedy."

Quayle looked rattled. Although George H. W. Bush and Quayle were to defeat Michael Dukakis and Bentsen in the election, the debate is remembered for that impressive response. That may or may not have been an unprepared remark by Bentsen but it communicated an important message to the public and embarrassed Quayle.[2]

However, Bentsen really did not address the issue of experience that Quayle mentioned. Instead, he attacked the person. When communicating your message you have to be prepared to deal with personal attacks. If Quayle had understood the proper response to that question, he could have turned it to his advantage. I had the opportunity multiple times to deal with personal attacks and my response always was, "Thanks for demonstrating the argument from intimidation. When you can't deal with the issue, you attack the person. Looks like you concede the point."

Learning communication skills is critical for a leader. The ability to communicate effectively not only helps deliver a concise message with clarity, but can also save lives. It is not difficult to find examples of disasters caused by poor communication in the field of medicine or between air traffic controllers and airline pilots. Consider the example of a nurse who works with adults but is put in a pediatric intensive care unit and incorrectly reads the doctor's handwriting abbreviations, giving an adult dose of medication to a child. The worst airliner accident in history occurred at Tenerife in the Canary Islands on March 27, 1977, causing 583 deaths. It involved two 747 jumbo jets crashing into each other while taxiing in the fog because of a communication error involving the air traffic controller and the pilots of the two airliners.

Remember that every time a message is transmitted orally, especially with others carrying the message to its final destination, there is the risk of message scramble.

Message scramble is humorously portrayed in the 1994 movie *Johnny Dangerously*, starring Michael Keaton. In the mess hall of a prison, a verbal message is sent by Johnny's mother, Lil, and is transmitted from one prisoner to another.

> **Lil:** "Get this to Johnny on the grapevine: Vermin is going to kill Johnny's brother at the Savoy Theater tomorrow night. Got it?"
> **Polly:** "Got it."

On the following day the message is passed through five prisoners until it reaches Johnny. This is what the message is by the time Johnny hears it:

> **Prisoner 5:** "There's a message on the grapevine, Johnny."
> **Johnny:** "Yeah, what is it?"
> **Prisoner 5:** "Johnny and the Mothers are playin' 'Stompin' the Savoy' in Vermont tonight."

Johnny: "Vermin's going to kill my brother at the Savoy Theater tonight?"
Prisoner 5: "I didn't say that."
Johnny: "No, but I know this grapevine."

Unfortunately, outside of the movies, no one has the ability to decipher the scrambled message as Johnny did. Thus, it is important to learn how to craft a clear message and also use a backup system that documents the message and prevents scrambling of the words.

Written Communication

One method of conveying a clear message is through the written word. A clearly written (or typed) instruction eliminates message scramble and can prevent disasters and save lives in war. Clarity may prevent the accidental launch of a nuclear missile.

How does one learn to write clearly? In my opinion, the best book to start with is *The Elements of Style*, by William Strunk, Jr., and E. B. White. Strunk wrote what he called the "little book" for teaching at Cornell. White, his student and later a famous essayist and author of *Charlotte's Web* and *Stuart Little*, is the co-author of the revisions of this classic book on style.

Here is a critical message from the book:

Vigorous writing is concise. A sentence should contain no unnecessary words, a paragraph no unnecessary sentences, for the same reason that a drawing should have no unnecessary lines and a machine no unnecessary parts. This requires not that the writer make all his sentences short, or that he avoid all detail and treat his subjects in outline, but that every word tell.

But the message must not only be concise; it must also be clear. Strunk and White compare messages written in two different styles in order to demonstrate the importance of writing with specificity.

My favorite example from Strunk and White is a quote from George Orwell's essay entitled "Politics and the English Language." Orwell takes a well known verse from Ecclesiastes and shows what happens when it is rewritten in "modern English."

Ecclesiastes: I returned, and saw under the sun, that the race is not to the swift, nor the battle to the strong, neither yet bread to the wise, nor yet riches to men of understanding, nor yet favor to men of skill; but time and chance happeneth to them all.

Modern English: Objective consideration of contemporary phenomena compels the conclusion that success or failure in competitive activities exhibits no tendency to be commensurate with innate capacity, but that a considerable element of the unpredictable must invariably be taken into account.[3]

Unfortunately, the latter type of writing shows up too frequently in modern day consultants' reports. It

is a sure way to bore the reader and invite misinter-
pretation of the true message. Specificity also may
evoke memories of personal experience and thus
enhance learning and retention of the message.

Other books that I strongly recommend are *The
Lively Art of Writing* by Lucille Vaughan Payne and
The Art of Styling Sentences by Marie Waddell, Robert
Esch, and Roberta Walker.

Among the tips in Payne's book are how to write an
essay, how to turn an opinion into a persuasive thesis,
and the importance of creating sentences that "sound"
pleasing. She emphasizes, as do Strunk and White,
the use of the active voice rather than passive voice in
sentence structure. Passive voice: "The car was driven
down Main Street." Active voice: "The car careened
down Main Street." Payne explains the passive voice
this way: "To avoid passive voice, make your subject
do something." Good advice and easy to remember.

In *The Art of Styling Sentences*, Waddell, Esch, and
Walker cite the importance of constructing sentences
in ways that will increase their impact and give them
a sense of style.

"You learn to write better sentences," the authors
say, "by writing just the way you learn almost every
other skill: by imitating the examples of those who
already have that skill." For practice, they offer twenty
sentence "patterns"—different literary devices and
arrangements of words or phrases—that good writers
have used to give their sentences rhythm or grace.

The book's pattern six,[4] for example, deals with the use of appositives, a technique that employs a series of words or phrases to describe or define another word or phrase. One example of the use of appositives in *The Art of Styling Sentences* is this: "The crack of the lion trainer's whip, the dissonant music of the calliope, the neighs of Arabian stallions—these sounds mean 'circus' to all children." In this sentence the words "crack," "music," and "neighs" are appositives, and each of the three words helps to define the word "circus" for children.

Another example is found in President Kennedy's inaugural address. This excerpt contains appositives for "enemies":

> Now the trumpet summons us again—not as a call to bear arms, though arms we need; not as a call to battle, though embattled we are—but a call to bear the burden of a long twilight struggle, year in and year out, "rejoicing in hope, patient in tribulation"—a struggle against the common enemies of man: tyranny, poverty, disease, and war itself.[5]

Note the use of the appositive pattern by Dr. Martin Luther King, Jr., in his famous "I Have a Dream" speech of August 28, 1963, where the appositives refer to "God's children":

> And when this happens, when we allow freedom to ring, when we let it ring from every village and

every hamlet, from every state and every city, we will be able to speed up that day when all of God's children, black men and white men, Jews and Gentiles, Protestants and Catholics, will be able to join hands and sing in the words of the old Negro spiritual:

Free at last! Free at last!
Thank God Almighty, we are free at last![6]

Another pattern that I frequently see in successful speeches is "parallel structure." As Payne points out, "A parallelism does not say the same thing in different words. The repetition is a repetition of structure."[7]

Again, let's look at President Kennedy's inaugural address: "Together let us explore the stars, conquer the deserts, eradicate disease, tap the ocean depths, and encourage the arts and commerce."

And don't forget the Brian Hooker translation of *Cyrano de Bergerac* by Edmond Rostand:

To sing, to laugh, to dream,
To walk in my own way and be alone,
Free, with an eye to see things as they are,
A voice that means manhood. ... [8]

All of the books I recommend identify the enemies of effective communication: vagueness, generalities, and jargon.

Public Speaking

A powerful speech can stir a crowd and establish a leader's credentials as an expert in his or her field. A boring speech, on the other hand, does not instill confidence in the audience that the speaker is a leader. Therefore, passion is a critical component of a powerful speech; audiences are tired of equivocators and monotonous speakers who read from printed speeches without eye contact.

One book that is outstanding for learning to deliver speeches is Thomas Montalbo's *The Power of Eloquence*. A subsequent edition titled *Public Speaking Made Easy* explains the "COD" of speechmaking: content, organization, and delivery.

The Language of Leadership

Over the years I have attended numerous lectures on speechwriting by Robert Friedman, a veteran speech-writing instructor. He teaches his students that public addresses can inform, persuade, motivate, and inspire their audiences—but you have to reach your audience before all those positive effects can happen. Friedman points out that—just as Cicero said—you want your audience to be attentive, receptive to your message, and well disposed to you. In short, you want them to like you. Here are a few suggestions to help you reach that goal:

- Create a common bond with the audience
- Compliment your audience
- Remember that stories of heroism tend to inspire audiences

Humor may also connect you with your audience, but be cautious. Few people can tell jokes well, and you run the risk of offending your audience if they take your jokes personally. For these reasons, self-deprecating humor is usually the most effective kind. Poke fun at yourself, not at your audience.

Moreover, Friedman maintains that effective leaders consistently send messages that are definitive and unequivocal. To this end, he stresses the importance of conveying a clear message. You should let your audience know why you are there and periodically remind them of your overarching purpose. Friedman speaks of six "Rs"[9] that will help you to communicate your message clearly:

"**R" 1:** Real: Speak English, not jargon. Don't say "interface," when you mean talk with each other. Don't use "maximize optimal results" when you mean sell all of the books in the store.
"**R" 2:** Repetition: Repeat important phrases.
"**R" 3:** Rhythm:

- Use variety: Vary your sentences in length and sentence pattern.
- Use balance.

  Example: Ask not what your country can do for you, but what you can do for your country.

  Example: Whether we bring our enemy to justice or justice to our enemy, justice will be done.
- Use the Rule of Threes: Group three related phrases or sentences in a logical sequence. Dozens of speeches, aphorisms, and proverbs provide examples of how effective using the Rule of Threes can be:

  Example: Friends, Romans, countrymen, lend me your ears.

  Example: I came, I saw, I conquered.

  Example: Blood, sweat, and tears

  Example: Will not tire, will not falter, will not fail …

  Example: Life, liberty, and the pursuit of happiness.

"R" 4: Rhetorical

Here are some rhetorical devices a speaker might use:

- Anaphora: The repetition of a word or phrase at the beginning of a series.

Winston Churchill: "We shall fight on the beaches, we shall fight in the fields and in the streets, we shall fight in the hills ..."
President Ronald Reagan: "These are the boys of Pointe-du-Hoc. These are the men who took the cliffs. These are the champions who helped free a continent. These are the heroes who helped end a war."

- Alliteration: Stringing together words that begin with the same letter or sound. ("A scientist who is sloppy in the lab, or sleazy in the market ...")

- Rhetorical question: How will I keep my medical practice open? Medicare continues to pay less and less and I am not allowed to charge the patient the remaining reasonable amount for my treatment. And what is the AMA doing about it?

"Rs" 5 and 6: Rock and Roll: Writing should be dynamic, vivid, and imaginative. Dynamic writing is a combination of concrete words and energetic verbs. NOT: Since we significantly improved our service efficiency, our profits have greatly increased. BUT: Since we cut installation time from two weeks to two days, profits have exploded.

Vivid writing engages all the senses. It include sounds, smells and textures as well as sights:

"The wards where we treat smoking's victims offer something less than the ads promise. You're surrounded not by lazy palms, but by colorless steel equipment. You smell not the honey of springtime, but the odor of alcohol. Your ears are filled not with jazz, but with buzzing machinery."

Be specific: Don't use "surgical instrument" when you can use "scalpel." Don't use abstractions such as "inflicted domestic violence" in place of "slapped," "punched around," etc.

Use energetic verbs, such as "jumped," "stared," "kicked," etc.

Be visual with language. Create pictures. Be sensual by engaging the senses.

Emulating the Masters

Another good resource is great speeches of the past. Many are recorded and are available in various formats. If you are able to access audio versions, pay particular attention to the speech's cadences and the effect on you. The Web site www.americanrhetoric. com contains what it considers the top one hundred American political speeches of the twentieth century, which can be read or listened to at the Web site.[10]

When I entered the race for a place on the board of the American Medical Association, I read all the inaugural addresses of the U.S. presidents. I found that some will put you to sleep. Others were very inspiring.

When reading speeches, try to discern what bores you and what excites you. If you can learn to think like your audience, you will be on your way to becoming an acclaimed speaker. The ability to communicate and inspire your audience to follow you is a very important aspect of leadership.

For practice, read these excerpts from the inaugural addresses of U.S. presidents William Howard Taft and John F. Kennedy and try to decide which one inspires you more.

Taft spoke the words below in March 1909—a time when there was no federal income tax in existence:

> In the mailing of a tariff bill the prime motive is taxation and the securing thereby of a revenue. Due largely to the business depression which followed the financial panic of 1907, the revenue from customs and other sources has decreased to such an extent that the expenditures for the current fiscal year will exceed the receipts by one hundred million dollars. It is imperative that such a deficit shall not continue, and the framers of the tariff bill must, of course, have in mind the total revenues likely to be produced by it and so arrange the duties as to secure an adequate income. Should it be impossible to do so by import duties, new kinds of taxation must be adopted, and among these I recommend a graduated

inheritance tax as correct in principle and as certain and easy of collection.[11]

By contrast, here are excerpts from the often-quoted inaugural address of President Kennedy:

> To those peoples in the huts and villages across the globe struggling to break the bonds of mass misery, we pledge our best efforts to help them help themselves, for whatever period is required—not because the Communists may be doing it, not because we seek their votes, but because it is right. If a free society cannot help the many who are poor, it cannot save the few who are rich. ... So let us begin anew—remembering on both sides that civility is not a sign of weakness, and sincerity is always subject to proof. Let us never negotiate out of fear. But let us never fear to negotiate. ... And so, my fellow Americans: ask not what your country can do for you—ask what you can do for your country. ... My fellow citizens of the world: ask not what America will do for you, but what together we can do for the freedom of man.[12]

Which speech did you find more inspirational? What makes that particular speech effective?

Provide the audience with examples of your vision and your principles—don't get bogged down with detailed statistics. An audience wants a visionary, not a bureaucrat. Regardless of the topic of your speech, you will seldom go wrong by assuming that your audience hopes for a better future.

I learned a lot from reading the inaugural speeches but I also learned from listening to recordings of my own public addresses. In reading, listening to, or watching your own speeches, you can pinpoint your weaknesses as a speaker. For example, you may not realize how frequently you say "er" or "uh" until you see or hear yourself on tape.

After a failed attempt in 1994 to be elected to the American Medical Association's board of trustees, I spoke with about 440 voters in the AMA house of delegates and asked them to evaluate my perfor-mance as a speaker. I told them I wanted the truth and my feelings would not be hurt by their candor. The most important lesson I learned from that expe-rience was to consider the perception of others when at the microphone. The impression they had received was that I would not be open to the views of others because I was so intense and did not smile. What a revelation!

When I ran again in 1996, I applied the lessons I had learned. I ran my speech by my peers beforehand and I smiled much more when I was at the podium. I won on the first ballot and was undefeated during my re-election campaigns.

Don't forget that when giving a speech, you should never exceed the time allotted. I keep a stopwatch on the podium. Do not look at a wristwatch on your arm, as this is distracting to your audience.

Finally, have some notes with you at the podium. You don't have to look at the three main points during the speech, but if you get stage fright and your mind goes blank, a quick glance at your notes will reboot your memory. Alternatively, having a memory aid will eliminate any possible anxiety about forgetting your message when the spotlight goes on. That happened to me when I was a young boy sent from my home in New Orleans to a boarding school in the country because of gang activity in my neighborhood.

The youngest boys the school accepted were fourth graders. I recently finished second grade and was put in fourth grade so I could enroll. The school chose me for a part in the Christmas play to boost my confidence.

There I was on the stage, the first speaker, with one paragraph to deliver. Suddenly the lights went off and a spotlight was on me. I froze and forgot the words. They removed me from the stage. No confidence builder that night!

My dad was in the audience and he came to me that night and said, "Don't worry. You'll be fine. I'm going to get you something that will prevent that from ever happening again." Soon afterward he brought me a reel-to-reel tape recorder and said, "Talk into this everyday after school and listen to yourself. Soon you'll never fear forgetting a speech." I did as he instructed and several years later became the ship's courageous doctor, Doctor Livesey, in another school play, Robert Louis Stevenson's *Treasure Island*. I remember vividly when we were invited to New Orleans and performed at a large school auditorium in my neighborhood. The lines I delivered in my role as the doctor still resonate in my mind. The captain of the ship pulled a knife on me and I responded, "Oh, you may go blustering high and wide when you go out to sea, but don't for a moment think you can also bluster me, for I am not only a doctor, Sir, but also a magistrate!"

When I finished my performance, my eyes caught my dad's eyes in the audience. He smiled and nodded his approval.

Communicating with the Media

"Be prepared" is the best advice I can give for deal- ing with the news media. If you have an interview scheduled, do your homework and try to anticipate the questions. If you get a message to call a reporter, call as soon as possible after your preparation. Those who are interviewed early in a reporter's research and writing are more likely to survive newspaper edits. If an editor has space for only 800 words and your com- ments begin in the last paragraph of a 900-word story, your comments won't appear in the published story.

Don't ramble when being interviewed. Know in advance the points you want to make and try to keep the number of points to three. No matter what the question, always be prepared to refer back to your three points. If the interviewer asks a question that is not relevant to the topic, point this out and return to the points you want to make.

When the public relations department of your company arranges an interview for you, ask if the company wants you to convey a specific message during the interview. Also request suggestions for the best, most succinct wording for accurate conveyance of that message. You may not have to use the exact recommended wording, but asking for it may inspire the department to think about points to be made during the interview. The PR department also may provide a helpful suggestion or two.

Videotaped television programs are always subject to editing, which means that in a televised debate, the best format is a live broadcast. Live programs may prevent having your words taken out of context. Most journalists are skilled and fair but some are more interested in sensationalism than fairness or accuracy, so be prepared to deal with this. Eternal vigilance is good advice when you are interviewed.

Your gestures and your personal appearance on television can affect how well your message is received by viewers. If the interviewer is on camera with you, look directly at him or her when answering questions.

Do not search for the camera with your eyes while talking. When you are at a location remote from the interviewer, look directly at the camera. Do not try to observe yourself on a TV monitor nearby. From the viewer's perspective, avoiding eye contact can suggest that you are evasive or lack honesty.

Always allow the television studio's makeup artist to prepare you for your time on camera. Never underestimate the power of makeup in certain circumstances—a makeup artist understands the color temperature of the studio lighting and the effect it will have on your natural facial coloration. He or she can make you look younger and fresher. During the years I was president elect, president, and immediate past president of the American Medical Association, I was frequently exhausted because of my travel schedule—249 days a year as president elect, 300 as president, and 250 as immediate past president. I went from city to city, country to country, doing interviews almost daily.

One night I was in Washington, D.C., for a major television debate on medical liability reform. I told the makeup artist I was exhausted, having gotten only three hours of sleep the night before, and that I would take a short nap while he worked. I mumbled that I probably would look tired on camera. He said, "Don't worry. I'll make you look young and alert tonight. How many years do you want removed?" I laughed and asked him to take ten years off.

The debate went very well. Afterward I got a call from my wife, who was visiting my mother. The two of them had concluded that I had won the debate, and they were impressed by how young I looked. That was high praise from two people who don't pull their punches when commenting on someone's appearance. This was when I became a believer in makeup for television appearances.

But what if you're in a studio that doesn't have a makeup artist? My wife solved that problem for me. She said the most important thing was to remove the shine from one's face, and recommended an oil-free gel that quickly dried as a powder. It comes in a small tube. It was simple to apply and eliminated the shine from my face.

One evening I was returning to New Orleans from one of my many trips to Washington, D.C. Just before I departed Ronald Reagan International Airport I got a call from a television host in New Orleans who wanted me on a program that night. The program was an important debate with someone who was on a national tour representing managed-care health plans, and the host did not want him on the show without an opposing viewpoint. I explained that it was not the best time for me, but he persisted and said he would meet me at the airport and take me directly to the studio.

It was a hot and humid New Orleans night, and when we arrived in the studio, all of us, including my debate opponent, were sweating. We were told the program would begin in two minutes. Then I had an inspiration. I excused myself and dashed to the rest-room. I washed my face with cold water, took from my computer bag the tube of gel my wife had given me, and applied it. The debate went well, but the response of the viewers was amazing. People called in to the TV station commenting that I looked so cool and fresh, and my opponent must have been badly rattled because he was dripping sweat.

Fans of political history remember the first-ever televised presidential debate in 1960 between then Senator John F. Kennedy of Massachusetts and Vice President Richard M. Nixon. Nixon was ill and did not use makeup. It was a disaster for him in the minds of TV viewers. Yet the radio listeners thought Nixon won. Erica Tyner Allen, writing for the Museum of Broadcast Communications, describes the circum-stances:

> (The) visual contrast was dramatic. In August, Nixon had seriously injured his knee and spent two weeks in the hospital. By the time of the first debate he was still twenty pounds underweight, his pallor still poor. He arrived at the debate in an ill-fitting shirt, and refused make-up to improve his color and lighten his perpetual "five o'clock shadow." Kennedy, by contrast, had spent early September campaigning in California. He was tan and confident and well

rested. "I had never seen him looking so fit," Nixon later wrote.

In substance, the candidates were much more evenly matched. Indeed, those who heard the first debate on the radio pronounced Nixon the winner. But the 70 million who watched television saw a candidate still sickly and obviously discomforted by Kennedy's smooth delivery and charisma. Those television viewers focused on what they saw, not what they heard. Studies of the audience indicated that, among television viewers, Kennedy was perceived the winner of the first debate by a very large margin.[13]

The bottom line is: Don't hesitate to take advice from people who are experts in makeup, and don't ignore the opinion of a wife.

Communicating in Meetings

> People who enjoy meetings should not be in charge of anything.
>
> —Thomas Sowell

The year was 1775, the place the Virginia House of Burgesses. The thirty-eight-year-old legislator looked around the room slowly and then began to speak. He had no notes. The majority in the chamber did not share his view of the crisis. But he knew well the implications for liberty if his position did not prevail. The pace of his words accelerated and his passion was unmistakable. He ended his oration with words that have echoed through the centuries: "Is life so dear, or peace so sweet, as to be purchased at the price of chains and slavery? Forbid it, Almighty God! I know not what course others may take; but as for me, *give me liberty or give me death!*"

The effect on the others was dramatic, and a chorus rang out: "To arms, to arms!"

Patrick Henry's oration swayed the group to vote for putting Virginia in a position of defense and arming Virginia troops to be ready to battle the British military. The vote was not unanimous. Henry won by a small margin, but win he did. No doubt other stirring comments in the speech that summarized the facts concisely contributed to the win. Here is an excerpt that illustrates the persuasiveness of his words:

> Mister President, it is natural to man to indulge in the illusions of hope. We are apt to shut our eyes against a painful truth, and listen to the song of that siren, till she transforms us into beasts. Is this the part of wise men, engaged in a great and arduous struggle for liberty? Are we disposed to be of the number of those who, having eyes, see not, and having ears, hear not, the things which so nearly concern their temporal salvation?
>
> For my part, whatever anguish of spirit it may cost, I am willing to know the whole truth—to

know the worst and to provide for it. I have but one lamp by which my feet are guided; and that is the lamp of experience. I know of no way of judging of the future but by the past. And judging by the past, I wish to know what there has been in the conduct of the British ministry for the last ten years, to justify those hopes with which gentlemen have been pleased to solace themselves and the House?

Is it that insidious smile with which our petition has been lately received? Trust it not, sir; it will prove a snare to your feet. Suffer not yourselves to be betrayed with a kiss. Ask yourselves how this gracious reception of our petition comports with these warlike preparations which cover our waters and darken our land. Are fleets and armies necessary to a work of love and reconciliation? Have we shown ourselves so unwilling to be reconciled that force must be called in to win back our love? Let us not deceive ourselves, sir. These are the implements of war and subjugation—the last arguments to which kings resort. I ask gentlemen, sir, what means this martial array, if its purpose be not to force us to submission? Can gentlemen assign any other possible motives for it? Has Great Britain any enemy, in this quarter of the world, to call for all this accumulation of navies and armies?

No, sir, she has none. They are meant for us; they can be meant for no other. They are sent over to bind and rivet upon us those chains which the British ministry have been so long forging. And what have we to oppose to them? Shall we try argument? Sir, we have been trying that for the last ten years. Have we anything new to offer on the subject? Nothing.

We have held the subject up in every light of which it is capable; but it has been all in vain. Shall we resort to entreaty and humble supplication? What terms shall we find which have not been already exhausted? Let us not, I beseech you, sir, deceive ourselves longer.[14]

Meetings do not often give birth to actions that change the course of history. More often than not they are ineffectual, causing many to feel—as Thomas Sowell states in the quote above—that those who enjoy meetings should not be trusted. Yet imagine the course of history if Patrick Henry had not shown up at that meeting in 1775.

Indeed, sometimes lightning strikes. Careful analysis shows that leaders who prevail know how to communicate and navigate the rules of meetings. No matter how worthwhile the cause, lack of preparedness leads to disaster. True leaders realize this and plan accordingly.

Leaders and potential leaders frequently resolve issues at meetings. Some gatherings are informal. Others are more formal committee meetings in which each member is asked to participate, but has no fiduciary responsibility. Still others are board meetings, in which each member has a fiduciary responsibility that requires the individual to act in the best interest of the organization. For all meetings, understand in advance the purpose of the meeting. For board meetings with fiduciary responsibility, insist on the agenda and the background materials well in advance so you can study and be prepared for the discussions.

Parliamentary Procedure

A complete discussion of the rules of the game should include the matter of parliamentary procedure. Any member of a board, a house of delegates, or a committee must know the applicable rules of parliamentary procedure just as a football player must know the boundaries of the playing field. It does no good to catch the football pass when you are standing outside the sideline, just as it does no good to make an outstanding oration in a meeting when the floor is not yours.

The first question you should ask is: Which rules are in use at your particular organization? (Are you operating under *Robert's Rules of Order* or *Sturgis' Standard Code of Parliamentary Procedure*?)

You should also find out whether the board or group has adopted any special rules.

It does not take long to learn how to introduce a resolution, and it is imperative that you do so. It is of no value to convince the other members of your position if there is no motion under discussion. Without a motion and a vote, the other members will just nod in agreement and move to the next topic. To get new policy or a new directive, there must be a motion and a positive majority vote.

The individual who does not know parliamentary procedure not only looks like a neophyte, but also seems unprepared. To be skilled in parliamentary procedure, to have done your homework, and to have reached a logical conclusion is akin to going into battle armed and with knowledge of the opponent's available tactics. Leaders today know this just as warriors of yesteryear learned how to ride horses and fire rifles accurately. Failure to do so increased casualties on their side.

During the 1970s I attended a meeting of over one hundred delegates to a state organization. I gave an impassioned plea for a resolution and it appeared I had won the day in debate—until another delegate went to the microphone and had the motion put in indefinite limbo. I did not know parliamentary procedure well enough to counter his motion. He won the day and my motion failed. It was embarrassing to me. Shortly after, an older doctor approached me and asked me to step outside the convention hall. He told me that my position was correct but I had lost because I did not know the rules of parliamentary procedure.

"Learn this," he said, "and this will never happen to you again."

When I returned home, I purchased the necessary books and never again had the experience of losing a debate because of parliamentary procedure. Years later, during a meeting of a national organization, that same doctor who beat me in parliamentary procedure in the 1970s was the speaker of the organization. He ruled my motion out of order. However, now familiar with the rules of the game, I explained my position to the house of delegates and used parliamentary procedure to ask for a vote of the assembly. I was thrilled to see the house of delegates vote in favor of my position and overrule the speaker. My point is that a leader must learn how to play by the rules; not doing so is a self-imposed handicap.

On critical issues, especially those that are controversial, make sure you have a written copy of any motion that gets passed. The sponsor of the motion can write the motion and hand it to the board chair, the house of delegates' speaker, or whomever is conducting the meeting prior to the vote so that there is no misunderstanding as to what was voted. The sponsor then must check the minutes and be certain that the exact wording has been documented. *He who controls the minutes controls the future of the organization.* It is amazing how many times resolutions are misquoted or absent in minutes when there is no written copy of the motion.

Lessons Learned

- Clear, unequivocal communication is necessary for strong leadership.
- A well-prepared, written message is less likely to be distorted by others.
- Great speeches of the past are a good place to learn about content, organization, and delivery.
- Learning rhetorical devices will make you a more effective writer and speaker.
- Preparation is the key for interviews and debates.
- Remain on topic during interviews.
- Practice makes perfect. Have notes available if your mind goes blank.
- Meetings can be a waste of time, but if led properly they can effect positive change.
- Knowing parliamentary procedure will help you to advance your ideas.
- Carefully monitoring the minutes of a meeting can prevent errors. The person who controls the minutes controls the future of the organization.

CHAPTER 9

CREATIVITY AND ACQUIRING THE STATE OF MIND NECESSARY FOR SUCCESS

Many highly intelligent people are poor thinkers. Many people of average intelligence are skilled thinkers. The power of a car is separate from the way the car is driven.

—Edward de Bono

For Louisiana's medical care industry, 1975 was a year of crisis. The cost of medical malpractice insurance had skyrocketed. Doctors feared that malpractice-insurance rates would make coverage unaffordable for them. One hospital administrator testified in a legislative committee, and repeated the same under oath in court years later, that his hospital had been offered a $1 million policy carrying a premium of the same amount.

During this time I was spending a lot of time in the state capitol building actively advocating changes in Louisiana's laws regarding medical liability insurance. One day, while waiting to testify before a legislative committee in favor of a piece of reform legislation, I was stopped outside the hearing room by someone who said, "I'm the state insurance commissioner. You're wasting your time. That bill [the one I was to testify about] will never pass. The trial attorneys are against it, labor is against it, and I'm against it." My answer was, "It surely is fortunate that we live in America and have freedom of speech and the right to petition government to change laws." Then I entered the hearing room and testified for the bill, which eventually passed and became law. This insurance commissioner did not fare so well. He later went to federal prison, as did the next two insurance commissioners.

Among the others working toward reforming the provisions of Louisiana's medical liability laws were the Louisiana State Medical Society and Dr. John Cooksey, an ophthalmologist from Monroe, Louisiana. Our efforts were rewarded with the passage of landmark legislation that I testified on. Much credit is due to Dr. Cooksey, who had the creativity to recommend a modification of a law that worked for the citizens of Indiana. That bill, H.B. 1465, became Act 817 of 1975. I recounted the history of that summer in Baton Rouge and praised Dr. Cooksey in an article for the *Journal of The Louisiana State Medical Society* on the twentieth anniversary of the passage of that landmark law.[1] It protected Louisiana from the effects of the medical liability crisis that later occurred in other states.

Because of my advocacy work in this regard, I was often approached for interviews or to write articles on the subject of medical liability insurance, suits without merit, countersuits, and loss of access to care for patients when a broken liability system existed.[2]

One of those requests came in 1984, while I was serving in Louisiana on the Governor's Commission on Medical Malpractice. The American Medical Association's division of state legislation asked me to write an article on Louisiana's medical liability law as amended in the 1980s for the AMA's state health legislative journal, which reported on new state legislation around the country. Because of time constraints connected with my medical practice, I agreed to do it providing I could send the manuscript close to the deadline by telephone, using a computer modem. This was, of course, before the prevalence of the Internet[3] or e-mail.[4]

The editorial staff in the AMA's state health legislation office told me that manuscripts had never been transmitted to AMA by computer modem and they had no idea how it could be done. I then spoke to the person in charge of their office's computers. "I just need to know the communication protocol settings," I said. He was intrigued by the idea. So we set the parameters for our modems to the same communication protocol, and I sent him a test transmission, which then appeared on his computer.[5,6] Again, this was not an e-mail program. I completed the article just before the deadline and sent it over a telephone line eleven years before I had an e-mail program. The episode probably will never appear in the AMA archives, but at the time the AMA's computer technicians told me this was the first time a manuscript was electronically transmitted to AMA in a format that was ready for use in their computers.[7]

• • •

You can't be limited by the way things are currently done. New discoveries and adoption of new technologies occur because some people elect to try a different way in the hopes of finding a better way. With a little encouragement, someone will always help make advances. He or she doesn't have to be the expert, but rather the person who dares to consider alternatives.

That knowledge helped me when I first served in the AMA house of delegates in the mid-1980s. On occasion, I realized I could win a debate if I had immediate access to reference material. During a debate, I would go to my hotel room on a lunch break, unscrew the mouthpiece of the phone, and attach two alligator clips to the internal phone wires as there was no modular jack on the outside of the phone. The other ends of the wires from the alligator clips were connected to my portable modem. Then I would set the communication parameters, and connect to the databases. I retrieved the information to a small battery powered portable laptop and went back to the debate with information that could not be challenged as I had copies of the original documents.

Now I can sit in meetings and use a wireless phone card in my laptop computer to instantly connect to the Internet. In the past twenty years, access to information has progressed exponentially. Creativity and paths to a destination make that possible. Emerging leaders need to recapture the curiosity they had as children.

Exploring creativity means getting rid of the concept of right and wrong answers. It doesn't mean ignoring ethics or the laws of physics and mathematics, but it does mean embracing the realization that, because everyone else is doing something one way does not make theirs the "right" way. The others may be doing a procedure the same way it has been done in the past but creative thinking can lead to an alternate idea that may prove to be faster, better, and cheaper.

A helpful book in beginning the search for creativity is Edward de Bono's *New Think*.

De Bono is an educator who teaches creativity and thinking as a skill. He has written many books, but I consider *New Think* a classic, and have recommended it to many audiences over the years.[8,9,10]

In the book, De Bono proposes that there are alternate paths to a destination. One of the principal concepts he puts forward is that of "lateral thinking," as opposed to "vertical thinking," as a means of generating new ideas.

To explain his views on lateral and vertical thinking, he tells the story of a young woman whose father owed money to another man. The man who lent the money said he wanted the young girl's hand in marriage. The young woman begged her father not to agree to this. Ultimately, against his daughter's wishes, the father agreed to a contest with the moneylender.

The rules were that the moneylender would hide a black pebble in one hand and a white one in the other. The daughter had to choose a hand. If the hand she chose held a black pebble, the debt would be forgiven, but the girl had to go through with the marriage. If the hand with the white pebble was chosen, the debt was forgiven and there would be no marriage.

The young woman saw that the lender cheated by hiding black pebbles in both hands. She knew if she exposed him, her father would lose his farm because he had no money to pay the debt. She selected one hand and the lender transferred the pebble to her hand without it being seen. She fell to the ground, opening up her hands to break the fall, and the chosen pebble fell among hundreds of others. She said she was sorry but not to worry, because the color of the pebble remaining in the lender's other hand had to be the opposite color of the pebble she had selected, which had fallen to the ground. Because the lender held a black pebble in each hand, and did not want to be caught cheating in front of all the witnesses who came to observe, he lost the contest and the father kept the farm. De Bono's lesson is that when a situation appears hopeless, consider alternative ways to attain the desired outcome. When you are faced with circumstances like those facing the young woman in the story, consider the flip side of the option before you.[11]

Two other books that teach how to enhance innovative thinking are Roger von Oech's *A Whack On The Side Of The Head* and *A Kick In The Seat Of The Pants*. Von Oech praises the words of the ancient Greek philosopher Heraclitus, whom he considers the world's first creativity teacher. He presents ten impediments to creativity, such as trying to find the "right" answer (implying that some believe there is only one possible solution), strictly adhering to

logical thinking, following rules, and adopting the
"that's not my job" attitude many people unfortunately live by. He describes these as mental "locks,"
and he strives to give you the keys to them. The word
"whack" in the title might refer to your being fired
from your job. You then are forced "at least for the
moment—to think something different." One might
consider changing careers and doing something that
really is different and exciting. *A Kick In The Seat Of
The Pants* discusses the four roles of the creative process. Von Oech identifies these roles as those of the
explorer, the artist, the judge, and the warrior. The
explorer might look in other fields for the answer.
The artist takes information and tries to use it to create new ideas. The judge evaluates a new idea and
decides if it is worthwhile. The warrior's role is to
take the idea and put it into action.[12]

Von Oech maintains a Web log he calls *Creative
Think* in which he offers such observations as "Creative thinking means not only generating new ideas;
it also means escaping from obsolete ones as well."
He also says, "We learn by our failures. Our errors are
the 'whacks' that lead us to 'think something different.'"[13] One might say this is not revolutionary. But
keep in mind the winning coach frequently says the
players must not only learn the basics but also imple-
ment them in a game.

The benefit of reading such books is that they serve
to remind you that you needn't be locked into doing

things the way they've always been done. With a little practice using the principles in these self-help books, you will enhance your problem solving skills, and you may be amazed at your awakening creativity.

Thus, those who aspire to be leaders must acquire the state of mind necessary for successful completion of a mission, and build up the confidence in themselves and in others that is necessary to be trusted with a leadership position. Individuals who courageously seek a new path distinguish themselves from the crowd.

A leader also learns to discern rumor from fact. Sometimes, validating the facts is difficult. But hearsay ought to be considered rumor unless it is validated.

Great discoveries frequently are made by new voices and contrarians. Leaders are not afraid of failure. Failure can be an important teacher. Thomas Edison needed to find a filament that would not immediately burn up when electricity was transmitted to it in a glass bulb. He did not consider each burning of the different filaments a failure, as he tested over a thousand filaments searching for one that would not burn. He considered each test a success, because it proved the burned filament was not the ideal one. For him it was all a matter of attitude, observation, and persistence. Finally he discovered that a piece of carbonized sewing thread, bent into a horseshoe shape and placed inside a bulb in a vacuum, would glow for 100 hours. He first demonstrated the electric lights in Menlo Park, New Jersey, on New Year's Eve in 1880. Trial and error led him to the invention that revolutionized electrical power systems and, in 1882, lit up one square mile in the Wall Street area of New York City.[14]

So, the creative person is a risk taker, but carefully considers what could go wrong and is prepared to deal with the complications. The leader learns from failure and tries to understand the system that set a person up for error rather than looking for scapegoats. Failure to fix the system means the error will occur again with someone else.

Lessons Learned

- Intelligence is important in leadership, but skilled thinking is critical.
- Fostering creativity is an important enhancement to logical thinking.
- A state of mind that welcomes curiosity, tries new approaches, and learns from error is a favorable approach to leadership development.
- Reading books on creativity generates new ideas and expands innovative possibilities.
- Always consider alternative paths to the same destination.
- A person who courageously seeks a new path is easily distinguished from the crowd.
- Leaders are not afraid of failure; they see it as a teaching experience.
- Leaders focus and do not waste time on unimportant activity.

CHAPTER 10

INTERPERSONAL RELATIONSHIPS

Piglet sidled up to Pooh from behind. "Pooh!" he whispered. "Yes, Piglet?" "Nothing," said Piglet, taking Pooh's paw. "I just wanted to be sure of you."

—A. A. Milne

Too often problems in communication thwart emerging leaders. Communication problems occur in the workplace and in the home. A failure to communicate can create stresses in the relationships with those you work or live with. This, in turn, adds stress to the potential leader's life and diverts her from focusing on the vision or goal.

Compassionate communication is the effective simple secret to enhance communication. It is easy to understand but not easy to accomplish in the heat of the moment. Let's use a married couple trying to resolve a problem to illustrate the point.

The wife is upset and, with an emotional outburst, accuses the husband of causing the problem. The husband concludes through simple logic that the wife is clearly wrong and he can prove this without difficulty. For him, the logical response would be to interrupt the wife and point out why she is wrong. In a computer program this is the logical way to fix a flaw in the incorrect thinking of the original programmer who inserted incorrect code. However, in this human interaction between two people, the husband's self-righteousness causes an escalation in the emotional outburst that is akin to throwing gasoline on a fire or causing a computer to crash.

In this situation, both the husband and the wife need to engage in compassionate communication. Practicing compassionate communication calls for them to approach the situation in three ways. The first is for both people to listen with full attention without interrupting. The second is for the husband to offer the wife a sincere statement of understanding, such as *"I understand why you are upset and I believe if I were in your situation I would not have handled the stress as well."* The third approach is for the husband to ask, *"What can I do to help?"* And to say it in a way that shows his wife that he really means it.

Accomplishing these three things enhances a relationship like a magic spell. Taken together, the three approaches demonstrate empathy and compassion. The offended person receives validation for the feelings he or she is having, and the offer to help quenches the raging fire.

Remember: Short-term gains or Pyrrhic victories are not the goals of a loving marriage or a friendship. Refusal to listen, correcting errors made during an emotional upset, or trying to win with "scorched earth" retaliation is destructive to a long-term relationship. Win-win is the aspirational ideal, and compassionate communication is the means to that end. The rewards are great in personal relationships, and there are spin-off benefits in all endeavors that call for personal interaction. In the business world, reduction of negative stress enhances creativity. This may lead to better products and a rise in the price of the company's stock because of increased sales!

I learned about compassionate communication from a psychologist many years ago. I wish that revelation had occurred earlier, as I can see myself as a young man, in a time-sensitive situation, not letting another person finish speaking before saying what I believed was the "correct" resolution of the conflict. But, as the old saying goes, "Better late than never." I continue to be a student of this powerful tool to improve interpersonal relationships. Some may have this wisdom in the recesses of their brains' hard drives but, as a consultant in risk management in the medical field, I always follow my cardinal rule in managing risk; namely, to *anticipate* what could go wrong and be prepared to handle it. Even though you may remember this rule, you have to be on guard not to forget it under stress.

Learning to Listen

People like to be appreciated. One way they believe they're appreciated is by receiving a signal that others value what they say. Paying attention while someone is speaking sends a valuable message. Others must learn how to listen rather than simply hear. Learning to listen rather than just hear requires being an active listener.

Being an active listener is not multitasking but rather giving full attention to the speaker, getting his or her meaning, and conveying that you understand what has been said. The active listener maintains eye contact with the speaker and indicates that the message is being evaluated. Nodding or some other subtle gesture can do this. At the end of the message you can comment, when appropriate, and rephrase the message to indicate that you understood it. For example, you might say, "What I hear you saying is you are working longer hours and not getting any extra compensation for your higher productivity." The response doesn't have to indicate agreement or disagreement. It merely confirms you heard the message correctly. Oftentimes, an upset speaker is looking for support while he or she airs a gripe. The speaker may not be asking for a solution to some problem and one should be cautious about being judgmental or offering a solution unless it is requested.

While at work, be careful that a co-worker doesn't dump a problem on your desk even if you are the supervisor. Listen to the message, and then ask the colleague what are the alternative ways to reach a solution. Then ask him or her to pick the best approach, use it, and report back later on the progress, unless you decide you want to approve it first.

Dealing with People in Top Positions

To confirm how concerned we all are about worker-supervisor issues, one need only search the Internet for the word "bosses." This will produce a list of some 18 million Web sites containing the word, including such links as "Different types of bosses," "How to deal with bad bosses," "Ten nightmare bosses," and "Bosses from hell."

Our personal estimation of others is largely decided by our very subjective perceptions. A boss's evaluation of a worker—and vice versa—will depend greatly on what one considers the other's virtues and faults.

Someone with leadership potential analyzes the strengths and weaknesses of each manager, boss, or supervisor he or she encounters. Then a central decision must be made: Is it possible for me to work productively with this individual in this working environment without having to sacrifice principles or suffer humiliation or abuse? If the environment is unsuitable, then it is best to depart. The journey of life is short, and one must enjoy it to develop one's full potential on the path to leadership and happiness. This does not mean the journey will be stress free, but merely that the person should look forward to the challenges and potential accomplishments that each day brings without consciously staying in a hostile working environment.

Remember not to spring surprises on supervisors, bosses, or even board chairs during a group meeting. It is best to alert them of the matter privately in advance. That prevents embarrassing them or having them lose face.

I am amazed at how much progress can be made toward having your ideas implemented if you don't care who gets credit for the idea. Even if someone else takes credit, the realization eventually will occur to everyone that teams involving you have a high degree of success.

Also, when dealing with supervisors or bosses, tell the truth. Be trustworthy. If you missed a deadline or made an error, admit it and make a plan to remedy the problem.

It is important to be respectful and civil. This does not mean succumbing to intimidation. Never respond in kind to name-calling. Stick to the issue in a logical unemotional way. That is one of the paths to leadership.

Despite these cautions, never forget that some people crave power and believe their feelings of poor self-worth can be overcome by exercising power over others and having their names emblazoned on buildings. They fail to learn the lessons of history, like the one captured in Percy Bysshe Shelley's poignant 1818 poem, "Ozymandias":

> I met a traveller from an antique land
> Who said: Two vast and trunkless legs of stone
> Stand in the desert. Near them on the sand,
> Half sunk, a shatter'd visage lies, whose frown
> And wrinkled lip and sneer of cold command
> Tell that its sculptor well those passions read
> Which yet survive, stamp'd on these lifeless things,
> The hand that mock'd them and the heart that fed
> And on the pedestal these words appear:
> "My name is Ozymandias, king of kings:
> Look on my works, ye mighty, and despair!"
> Nothing beside remains: round the decay
> Of that colossal wreck, boundless and bare,
> The lone and level sands stretch far away.[1]

Note how people respond to you when you are in power and out of power.

Observe candidates for public office. Note the attention they pay to you before they're elected and afterward, whether or not they win or lose. If you notice that a candidate is solicitous when campaigning but ignores you after the election, you have identified someone who is not a leader.

If you have been elected to an office, note the people who try to befriend you, and then observe them when you are no longer in office. If you note that they ignore you, you have identified those who were interested only in what you could do for them while you were in office.

If, during a conversation with a candidate at a political event, you notice that he or she is constantly looking beyond you to see whom he or she can approach next, it is unlikely that the candidate will impress you with his sincerity in the long term.

Sincerity is personified in a couple who have been dear to me since high school. They invited my wife and me to a private wedding of their daughter to a man of great wealth. They told me they had invited the same people to the wedding as they would have invited if their daughter had married a garbage man. They are sincere friends of true worth.

Selecting Associates or Members of Your Team

Achieving one hundred percent accuracy in choosing outstanding associates is difficult. A good rule is to hire people who impress you with their intelligence and problem-solving skills. Seek people who can teach you something or add skills missing in the organization. I always try to associate myself with people who can teach me something. We always should be students and seek gifted teachers. Look for people who are pleasant. Avoid sarcastic, negative people. Always check references at the primary source. If the resume indicates a college degree, call the college and verify. Don't rely on secondary sources. It is amazing how many people alter their curriculum vitae and add false information. More amazing is how many companies fail to verify credentials at the source.

Lessons Learned

- Remember the three critical points of compassionate communication:

  1. Learn to be an active listener.
  2. Validate the feelings of others in a discussion.
  3. Ask how you can help after listening to someone who is upset.

- Before any meeting with your boss attended by others, alert him or her to any facts that are crucial to issues on the agenda.
- Practice civility but never compromise your principles.
- Never lose the common touch by letting status change you.

- Learn to distinguish between friends and opportunists.
- Select associates on merit and always verify credentials from primary sources.

There were strong opinions about the performance of the mayor in the aftermath of Hurricane Katrina. (©2007 by Steve Kelley of the *The Times-Picayune*. Reproduced with permission.)

Few officials escaped criticism after Hurricane Katrina. (©2005 by Mike Lukovich of Creators Syndicate. Reproduced with permission.)

Signs at a business on St. Charles Avenue after Hurricane Katrina floodwater subsided in September 2005.

Dr. Palmisano delivers one of the emergency communicators donated by The Doctors Company to the French Quarter Health Department in Exile, started by Dr. Brobson Lutz.

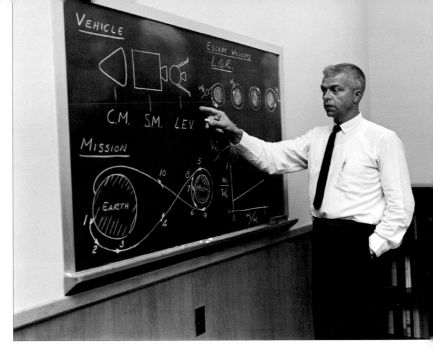

John C. Houbolt, July 24, 1962, showing his space rendezvous concept for lunar landings. Lunar Orbital Rendezvous (LOR) would be used in the Apollo program. (NASA image used with permission.)

The July 16, 1969 liftoff of the Apollo 11 Saturn V space vehicle, manned by astronauts Neil A. Armstrong, Michael Collins, and Edwin E. Aldrin, Jr., resulted in the first successful landing of humans on the moon. (NASA image used with permission.)

Governor-elect Bobby Jindal at campaign headquarters in Baton Rouge when the election results were announced on October 20, 2007.

Dr. Palmisano with China's Minister of Health, Zhu Chen, MD, PhD, in Shanghai, 2008, the night before the fifth Sino-U.S. Symposium on Medicine in the 21st Century. Dr. Zhu Chen's pioneering work in leukemia therapy is described in chapter 16.

PAID THE SUPREME SACRIFICE

FREEDOM IS NOT FREE

Dr. Palmisano took this photo at the Korean War Memorial on Veterans Memorial Blvd. in Metairie, Louisiana shortly after the terrorist attack on America, September 11, 2001. The reflection of the flags at half-mast reinforced the sadness of the times.

A February 12, 1998 cartoon by Pulitzer Prize-winning editorial cartoonist Jeff MacNelly. (© 1998 by *The Chicago Tribune.* Reproduced with permission.)

Lieutenant Commander Paul Galanti, U.S. Navy pilot, meeting his wife in the United States following his 1973 release from the infamous "Hanoi Hilton." (From *Newsweek,* February 26, 1973. ©1973 by Newsweek, Inc. All rights reserved. Used by permission and protected by the copyright laws of the United States. The printing, copying, redistribution, or retransmission of the Material without express written permission is prohibited. Photograph used with permission from Don Carl Steffen/Photo Researchers.)

Henry W. Giles, MD in 2008 at his home in Baton Rouge, Louisiana. Read about his heroic actions in chapter 16.

Dr. Henry Giles received this gift from the 134th Medical Detachment.

This painting depicts Ranger hero Leonard Lomell aiming his weapon after climbing the cliffs of Pointe-du-Hoc in Normandy on D-Day, June 6, 1944. (© 2006 *The Point* by Larry Selman. Reproduced with permission.)

A JCOC 63 lapel pin, worn to honor the brave men and women in the U.S. volunteer armed forces, an incubator for leadership. Dr. Palmisano received this pin after nine days of maneuvers with the military as one of sixty American "opinion leaders" chosen by the Department of Defense.

Dr. Palmisano at the start of the Joint Civilian Orientation Conference (JCOC 63), April 29, 2000, with Secretary of Defense William S. Cohen.

CHAPTER 11

FINDING TRUTH

In a time of universal deceit, telling the truth becomes a revolutionary act.

—George Orwell

I walked into the lecture hall to make a presentation as I had done hundreds of times before on many different topics, in front of large and small audiences, sometimes speaking to millions on prime-time television programs. But tonight would be different. Four other speakers were on the patient safety panel.

I decided not to say anything until the question and answer period began. When I was called on to speak by the moderator, I declined, saying that instead I would let a nine-minute documentary video speak for me. I noted the questioning glances in the audience.

The lights went down and the video began. A few minutes into it I could feel tears welling up in my eyes, and I saw others wiping theirs. After the question and answer period, every panelist asked me for a copy of the video. It is available from the online store of the Institute for Safe Medication Practices.[1] The title of the documentary is *Beyond Blame*. It tells the true stories of three people in the medical field. Each played a role in the death of at least one patient, not with intent but by error. All of those involved had outstanding records as competent, compassionate professionals.

In the video a nurse explains how she injected a lethal dose of concentrated potassium chloride directly into a patient's vein. She meant to administer the diuretic drug ordered by a physician in an attempt to alleviate the patient's worsening condition. The diuretic removes excess fluid in a patient suffering from congestive heart failure and other conditions.

Potassium in small amounts is necessary for health. But in concentrated form, it is lethal when rapidly injected intravenously. Before concentrated potassium chloride is injected, a small vial of it is mixed with a liter of liquids and administered over a period of eight hours.

In the case described in the documentary video, the patient's heart stopped beating after the lethal injection, and an attempt at resuscitation failed. At the patient's bedside, among the other drugs used in the resuscitation, was an open, empty vial bearing a label that identified its former contents as concentrated potassium chloride. This was the moment when the nurse realized a fatal mistake had been made.

In another tragic case depicted in the video, a hospital pharmacist explained how one day he reached up and removed from a shelf an antibiotic that had been stored at the same spot on the shelf for years, and which he then diluted in a solution and sent out to nurses for intravenous injections. However, someone who restocked the pharmacy had mistakenly placed on the shelf space packets that resembled the antibiotic packets but contained a paralyzing agent. Two patients died before the mistake was discovered.

A third case concerned a boy in an operating room ready to be anesthetized for a relatively minor ear operation. After he received the injection, he suddenly became very ill and eventually died. An analysis of all medications that had been in the operating room showed that, rather than the local anesthesia, the boy had been administered a lethal dose of epinephrine, a vasoconstrictor. The boy's family was told of the error and, on the same day, a settlement was reached between the parents and the hospital with the family's attorney present. The family thanked the nurse who was the hospital risk manager for telling them the truth so they could go on with their lives.

As the caregivers tell their stories, their pain is obvious. You see their difficulty in talking about their experiences, and their sadness for what happened to the patients. You note hand wringing as some of them speak.

In the first two stories there was the shame-and-blame response that dictates the person who makes a mistake is punished rather than fixing the systems that lead to the error. The pharmacist was told to quit and the nurse had to deal with the licensing board. In the video the nurse says that for years she could not talk about this painful experience without becoming physically ill.

Fortunately, all of these medical professionals had the courage to tell their stories. The family of the boy who was given the wrong medication allowed his name to be used in the video for the promotion of patient safety. The incident in which the boy died and other such occurrences led to the formation of the National Patient Safety Foundation, on whose board of directors I served as a founding member for nine years and now serve on its advisory board of governors.

The goal of patient safety efforts is to fix systems that lead to errors like those described in the video. Another aim is to get rid of shame and blame and attempts to hide what happened when errors occur. A system fix for the episode concerning concentrated potassium chloride is to remove it permanently from the nursing station and have such medications diluted exclusively in the pharmacy.

In a different example not in the video, the system fix for an error in connecting the gaseous anesthesia line to the oxygen line is to change the connectors so that one is square and one is round, making it virtually impossible to connect the two. Alerts about system errors such as this one can be found in the "Sentinel Events" link at the Web site of The Joint Commission, an agency that sets standards for the country's health care industry.[2]

Unfortunately, when complications occur such as a deep venous thrombosis in a leg vein that moves to the lungs and causes death through no error of the medical personnel, there is always the risk of a malpractice suit alleging negligence. Such an occurrence can happen in the absence of negligence. These are expensive to defend. Eighty percent of medical malpractice lawsuits are closed without payment of any money to the person suing. Among cases that go to trial, physicians win eighty-nine percent of the time. This says something about the lack of peer review among attorneys or appropriate scrutiny by the legal system for suits filed. If a suit is declared to be without merit, there is almost no chance of either a successful countersuit by the defendant or sanctions by the judge against the plaintiff. Society must devise a way to hold accountable those who file suits without merit. The responsibility should fall on the legal professional to evaluate the merits of a case properly. Failure to do so should cause the attorney at fault to be held accountable. Harm is done to those who are sued without justification. The lure of a big jackpot or large settlement causes this out-of-control litigation system to hamper the economic engine of the United States and, in the medical situation, increase the risk that a needed specialist will not be available in one's hour of need. I gave examples of such unavailability of physicians in multiple forums, including an article in the November/December 2004 issue of *The Saturday Evening Post* and in peer-reviewed medical journals.[3]

Some complicated instances of medical treatment can significantly increase the probability that a patient will sue. One example is this scenario: A woman in labor arrives at an emergency room. She has no physician and has not seen any physician during her pregnancy. The woman is experiencing medically important complications because she has not seen a physician for prenatal care and perhaps she has been using illicit drugs. A child is born neurologically impaired. The child will require long-term medical care. The woman sees an attorney who predicts a large settlement because it is a sympathy case.

Even when the physicians and nurses at the hospital do everything possible and meet the highest standard of care, the probability that a sympathetic jury will award the plaintiff a large sum of money is a significant possibility. Most attorneys who represent the plaintiff in such cases charge a contingency fee of thirty-three-and-one-thirds percent of the award if the case is settled out of court. Others charge forty percent if the case goes to trial and fifty percent if the court's decision is appealed. In some instances the plaintiff's attorney not only receives a large percentage of the money awarded by the court, he or she also receives the cost of all trial-related expenses from the client's share of the award. In some cases the attorney ends up with more money than the patient.

During my many years of debating with attorneys at meetings and on television, no one has been able to challenge successfully that money scenario.

Those who aspire to be leaders in America need to fix the broken medical liability system so that access to medical care remains available in one's hour of need. There needs to be a change so that the truth can be uncovered as soon as possible without finger pointing, shame and blame, and lengthy litigation. Of course there should be accountability but not the failed methodology now used. The federal Patient Safety and Quality Improvement Act of 2005 was an important step, with great potential to make medicine safer. Under that law, physicians, nurses, and hospital staff confidentially report errors to patient safety organizations. Experts then review the reports and recommend system changes to prevent repetition of the error. All of the information is entered in a nationally accessible database to help prevent the error from happening elsewhere. All personal references are deleted before any information joins the database. Unfortunately, two and a half years after the law was passed, the required regulations had not been finalized to allow the system to start functioning.

The American Medical Association, The Joint Commission, and the National Patient Safety Foundation recommend that patients who were affected by errors be told of those errors. There is no valid reason—including the fear of litigation—to withhold such information.

I have participated in many public forums sponsored by the National Patient Safety Foundation. Repeatedly, I saw people take the microphone and say that, when something bad happens to a loved one in a hospital, they first want to know why it happened. Then, they want to know what is being done to prevent this from happening again to someone else. And, finally, that it would be nice to hear that the person responsible for the error is sorry. In many states, laws make it easier for those responsible to express their remorse by eliminating the fear that such statements will be used against them in court. Sometimes, no one knows the exact circumstances that led to the error. Still, it is always possible to express concern or apologize. Assuring an affected family that an error will be fully investigated, and that all of the findings will be shared with the family is the kind of openness that builds trust. In the *Beyond Blame* video, the actions taken after the boy was given a lethal injection offer a good example of how candor and immediately informing the boy's parents of the investigation's findings prevented a potentially lengthy and costly litigation.

The quest for truth is sometimes a difficult undertaking. One example is the role of the trial juror as he or she listens to both sides advance different versions of events. Many times it comes down to the credibility of witnesses when evidence is equivocal.

Consider the difference between a trial lawyer's questions in court and a scientist's search for a new discovery. As many lawyers who do trial work have told me, a lawyer never asks a question during a trial without knowing the answer. A scientist never asks a question he or she already knows the answer to.

When a trial lawyer asks a witness a question, he is trying to destroy the credibility of the opposition witness. After asking the question he may read a conflicting statement the witness made earlier in a deposition and ask, "Are you lying now or when you gave the deposition?" Many trial lawyers tell me the goal in a trial is to win, not to find the truth, and that truth is what the jury says it is.

In my lectures to physicians, nurses, and medical students I stress the importance of documenting events in the treatment of a patient as soon as possible after any procedure. When a surgeon completes an operation, he or she should record the important details without delay. Also, while waiting for the report to be entered in the chart, the surgeon should add a handwritten note to the chart to record what was done in the interim. A trial jury is more likely to accept as reliable evidence any data that was recorded immediately after the fact than data that was entered a week later. I call this advice the CATO rule. Complete, Accurate, Timely, and Objective. I also add it should be legible!

For a leader, the pursuit of truth requires more than just reading the newspaper, watching television news reports, or searching the Internet. Errors abound in those media. Some result from poor research, and others stem from bias or an agenda. A leader does more than scan information from these sources. When obtaining correct information is critical, verification from primary sources is especially necessary.

A leader needs to know that unreliable samples and statistics are misleading. Here is an example of what can happen: I once checked a Web site for information about the types of errors that can occur when statistical data is being used. The site contained helpful information on such errors. However, one example the site gave regarding the identity of the person who solved the etiology of a cholera epidemic in London in the nineteenth century was not accurate. Chadwick and Farr were incorrectly identified as the solvers of the mystery surrounding a contaminated well pump. The truth is that Chadwick and Farr had put forth a wrong theory, claiming that contaminated air, or "miasma," was the cause of the epidemic and opposed the true discoverer, Dr. John Snow, who proved the cause was contaminated water. The site also gave 1831 as the year of the epidemic, when it actually occurred in 1853–1854. I told the story of Dr. Snow's pioneering work in chapter 4, "A Primer on 'Homework.'"

Information that is not peer-reviewed should be looked on with skepticism. Many times, information gotten from the Internet is not peer-reviewed yet is presented as fact rather than opinion.

So where can an emerging leader get some basic information about statistical errors? Take a course in statistics or visit university Web sites or search for peer-reviewed articles available online. Such study will introduce you to terms including mean, median, mode, average, normal distributions, non-normal distributions, and more. You can learn to watch out for inappropriate comparisons, improper sampling and lack of randomness of sample, and the importance of knowing such things as whether the results of a drug study show relative risk reduction rather than absolute risk reduction. For example, relative risk reduction statistics may falsely imply great improvement. As Susan Mayor said in the *British Medical Journal* in 2002, "If a disease kills two in every million people, a drug that reduces the death rate to one in a million would give a relative risk reduction of fifty percent, which appears to be a major benefit. However, the absolute risk reduction would only be one in a million."[4]

The "Math Talk" section of the Web site of "Hands-On Astrophysics," an educational project of the American Association of Variable Star Observers,[5] summarizes statistics as

> a powerful tool for uncovering truth; [but] when used improperly, it can be manipulated to prove almost anything. ... We have seen that if you want to deceive people, statistics makes it easy. In fact, even if you want to be honest, there are so many things that can go wrong in an experiment or a survey that we must carefully guard against bias. Even if we succeed, and get an unbiased result which is "statistically significant," it still might have happened just by accident. So the experiment has to be repeated, many times, and each time requires the same care in guarding against any bias which could affect the results.

In 2007, I attended the National Patient Safety Foundation Annual Patient Safety Congress where Dr. Peter Pronovost of Johns Hopkins University gave an outstanding presentation. He told the audience that initially his research showed that deaths from sepsis in an intensive care unit decreased sixty-nine percent when certain new procedures were used. That finding was published and hailed worldwide. However, he continued to study his statistics in great detail and discovered a sampling error that went unnoticed even by the reviewers of his paper. When he corrected the sampling error, his results showed no improvement at all. He was at the conference to tell the audience about the error and the importance of understanding and applying statistics correctly. If only we had more people like this honest researcher!

One of the most profound observations on statistics is attributed by Mark Twain to nineteenth century British Prime Minister Benjamin Disraeli. Twain writes: "Figures often beguile me, particularly when I have the arranging of them myself; in which case the remark attributed to Disraeli would often apply with justice and force: 'There are three kinds of lies: lies, damned lies, and statistics.'"[6]

Don't let anyone else frame the argument or limit the scope of discovery in the pursuit of truth and innovation. That advice holds true for debates. If you let someone else frame the issue, you will lose the debate. If you let someone limit the scope of discovery in research, you may never find the answer to the research question. Of course, there are legal limits to discovery in litigation to preserve certain recognized areas of confidentiality and to prevent prejudice.

Leaders must not only tell the truth but also pursue the truth when others conceal it. It is not an easy task but this is an important distinguishing feature of a leader. The pursuit of truth in the political arena is most challenging. As I listen to claims and counterclaims and spinmasters on television, I am reminded of George Orwell's dystopian novel,

Nineteen Eighty-Four, wherein the main character Winston Smith lives in a totalitarian state and works in the "Ministry of Truth." In that place history constantly is rewritten and evidence destroyed. Progress never will occur with such activity. Freedom, liberty, the rule of law, and truth are the keys to progress. Without truth, a people, a state, a country withers like a plant without water. As Winston Churchill said, "The truth is incontrovertible. Malice may attack it and ignorance may deride it, but in the end there it is." It is up to leaders to seek it out. The electorate cries out for such authentic leadership.

Such action earns credibility for the leaders and gives others the incentive to be followers. Recall John 8:31–32, "and the truth will set you free."

Lessons Learned

- Leaders are truthful.
- Pursue truth no matter how difficult the task.
- Timely documentation of events decreases the risk of disputes later as to what really happened.
- In the quest for truth, don't let others frame the debate or limit it.
- Obtaining truth and fixing flawed systems does more good than "shame and blame."
- Verify information from Internet sources because errors abound.

- Gain a working knowledge of statistics so you can identify misleading or statistical conclusions with bias.
- Being truthful earns respect and credibility and gathers followers.

CHAPTER 12

FINANCIAL CONSIDERATIONS AND FIDUCIARY RESPONSIBILITY

With great power comes great responsibility.
—*Spider-Man*'s Uncle Ben

Financial Reports and Investments that Board Members Oversee

Among the fiduciary responsibilities of people serving on boards of directors is the oversight of financial reports and investments. To gain additional insight and advice for emerging leaders, I spoke with three financial experts about how to enhance the skill of board members when they are called upon to evaluate the performance of the people they hire to manage the financial assets of their organization.

In 2008, I interviewed Randall K. Zeller, managing director of RBC Public Fund Services, a municipal asset management company whose work includes managing the money that cities, counties, and other municipal entities receive from the bonds they issue.

To provide a model for his observations, Zeller chose the board of an insurance company. Here are some of his comments:

The financial assets of some insurance companies can add up to billions of dollars, making them a leading segment of the universe of institutional investors, who have very large amounts of money at their disposal to pour into stocks, bonds and markets.

When a company's officers or board members are hiring or evaluating the performance of those who manage their financial assets, they must ask them a number of basic questions to be sure that the complexities and responsibilities involved in the effort, and the need to provide reliable guidance, are understood. Are officers and board members satisfied that the asset managers understand the company's basic business operations, business plans, regulatory environment and risk preferences? Do company executives and the asset managers understand the liquidity needs of the insurance company that employs them, the duration of its assets and liabilities, tax status and financial strength? How do asset managers allocate the chosen investments? Do they invest only in specific asset classes (e.g., stocks and bonds) or is their approach robust enough to include other permissible asset classes? Do managers understand investment regulations, rating agency consider- ations, liability and capital constraints, the competi- tive position and tax efficiency of their investment strategies.

Following these basic steps, officers and directors must be in a position to review their asset managers' work and understand if the managers are adhering to the company's strategic and tactical business operations. Do they review the managers' investment performance relative to appropriate benchmarks, market conditions and evolving business dynamics? As fiduciaries, all parties to the process must be on their game at all times.

Good insurance-company asset managers, in conjunction with officers and directors who are well versed in these concepts, stand a very good chance of investment strategy contributing to the success of the insurance enterprise.[1]

Dave Preimesberger, chief financial officer of The Doctors Company, gave me this advice in 2007 for board members who wish to enhance their under- standing of the financial reports they must review:

1. Board members should get "financially" educated. Universities and The Conference Board,[2]
   a business-supported, nonprofit educational
   company for executives, are but two of the many
   sources of good one- and two-day educational
   programs covering general finance and finance
   and accounting for the non-financial executive.
2. Board members would be well served schedul-
   ing an afternoon with the chief financial officer
   or other company executives (internal audit,
   human resources, operations) to learn more
   about the business. The CFO could review the
   company's financials and provide an overview
   of the financial dynamics of the organization.
   Some companies (including The Doctors Company) have formal or informal programs for
   board members to learn about the business by
   meeting with company officials and reviewing
   specially prepared information packages (the
   history of the company, industry data, market
   environment, competitor analysis, etc.).
3. Board members should be encouraged to attend
   committee meetings (finance, audit, governance, regulatory, investment, etc.) that they
   are not assigned to. One can learn much from
   such activity and also learn from the questions
   other board members are asking.
4. As for specific financial information, board
   members should read thoroughly all quarterly

and annual reports published by the company and any other public filings. Spend time on the company's Web site reviewing historical annual reports and filings. There are wonderful financial resources for board members at the site of the American Institute of Certified Public Accountants (http://aicpa.org/) and, particularly in the area of corporate governance, at the Web sites of major accounting firms.

5. Board members shouldn't hesitate to ask questions in sessions to clarify issues and increase understanding. Management and staff expect questions, and they understand that board members who aren't involved day to day in the business will make such inquiries.

6. Budget and assumptions should be vetted and changes fully discussed. Significant departures from any plan should be explained in detail. Buzzwords and abbreviations (such as "WIP for "work in progress," "OTTI" for "other than temporary impairment," etc.) should be clearly defined. Perhaps written materials should include a glossary of terms, definitions, etc.[3]

Another expert who was an outstanding financial teacher for me during the years I served on the American Medical Association board of trustees was the AMA's chief financial officer.[4] Here a few of the important points I learned from her that apply to any company or organization.

When deciding if a product should be eliminated, one important matter to consider is its profitability. The cost of producing the item (the "variable costs," which include production, sales commissions, delivery of the product, etc.) is subtracted from the sales income. The remainder is divided by the sales income to get the margin percentage.

$$\frac{\text{Product Revenue} - \text{Product Variable Costs}}{\text{Product Revenue}}$$

For example, if a product brings in sales revenue of $100,000 but the expenses or all costs of the product are $75,000, then the profit is $25,000. Dividing $25,000 by $100,000 gives a margin of twenty-five percent. This percent can be compared to the margin percentage of other products to help decide which product, if any, should be eliminated. In many cases, fixed costs are allocated across multiple product lines, but cannot be eliminated when the product is "cut," creating a bigger problem than the one you started with. So the next step is to determine how much of the fixed costs, if any, assigned to the product will be eliminated.

Cash flow statements are very important because they are the starting point for calculating "free cash flow," as it is known on Wall Street. Analyze an organization's consolidated statements of cash flow by starting with net cash provided by operating activities [net cash of cash received and cash spent] less certain items (notes receivable and purchase of property and equipment) to get free cash flow. In other words, how much cash is available after money is spent maintaining or expanding the organization's assets. This "adjusted cash" is what is available to make new products, fund expansion (such as buying other companies) or pay dividends to shareholders.[5]

In the "free cash" calculation, sales of assets or other unusual or nonrecurring items are not included. Those are onetime events and not an indication of the money coming in from the company's primary ongoing activity.

This analysis helps in determining if a company's business plan is generating enough income from its products to ensure its future. This prevents a false impression that could occur when a company is just selling off its assets or engaging in other creative financing that can sometimes cover up operating problems.

The most important thing to remember regarding finances is to make sure that the financial report given to the board by management is consistent, makes sense, and the numbers add up to financial stability. Your CFO or finance manager is responsible for explaining things in a logical and understandable fashion—not to obscure issues with complicated, technical jargon. If something can't be explained easily, it may be time to get your own expert outside of the company to take a look and give a second opinion.

Finally, when an investment adviser addresses a board I'm a member of, I always want to know what his or her advice has yielded over the years compared to the approach given in a book that my surgical partner and financial wizard, Dr. James E. Brown, recommended to me many years ago. It is *Common Sense on Mutual Funds* by John Bogle, founder of The Vanguard Group of mutual funds and the originator of index investing. The book provides an effective immunization against the advice of anyone trying to turn you into a "day trader," one who buys and sells stocks and other securities daily, trying to take advantage of major moves in the markets. Those who try this remind me of an admonition my dad gave me while we were driving past a racetrack. "Son," he said, "the people who hang out here will end up barefoot in the winter and wearing old overcoats in the summer."

Fiduciary Responsibility

Fiduciary responsibility was the focus of renewed scrutiny after the WorldCom and Enron disasters. Congress responded and passed Sarbanes-Oxley in an attempt to reduce the risk of such debacles. Leaders study and learn the laws and their fiduciary responsibility early so that they do not function in ignorance. For example, the duties for members of boards of directors of nonprofit organizations are summarized in the following excerpts from Daniel L. Kurtz's book, *Board Liability*:

> Non-profit directors have the three commonly recognized duties to the organization: the duties of CARE, LOYALTY, and OBEDIENCE. The duty of CARE concerns the director's competence in performing directorial functions and typically requires him to use the "care that an ordinarily prudent person would exercise in a like position and under similar circumstances." The duty of LOYALTY requires the director's faithful pursuit of the interests of the organization he serves, rather than the financial or other interests of the director or of another person or organization. And the duty of OBEDIENCE requires that a director act with fidelity, within the bounds of the law generally, to the organization's *"mission"* as expressed in its charter and by-laws.[6]
>
> Directors may not abdicate their responsibilities and be relieved of potential liability simply by relying blindly on others or by delegating authority to board committees, officers, or other agents of the organization (for example, employees or outside experts). Reliance, to be effective, requires vigilance by the board so that material or advice relied on forms the basis of an informed judgment. In other words, a report must have been read, thought about, listened to, or otherwise assimilated and digested. A director can't properly rely upon a fund-raising consultant's

report if all the director knows is the report's conclusion–that would not be acting in "good" faith nor would it give sufficient means to evaluate the expert's performance. In most circumstances a director is entitled to rely on reports prepared by individuals or committees (assuming that their contents have been absorbed); where a director has a reasonable basis to be suspicious, the general duty of care requires the director to make further inquiry.[7]

Kurtz's book is a good starting place for someone who desires to learn more about being a fiduciary.

In response to a CEO or staff person or another board member who says we must trust them, the correct response is, that is not allowed in the role of a fiduciary unless we have honored the requirements mandated for trustees listed by Kuntz.

Because of a trustee's fiduciary responsibility, blind trust is not an option; a blind trust standard makes trustees unnecessary. The trustee has the obligation to carry out the duties of care, loyalty, and obedience. It is not a thoughtless "rubber-stamp" position.

In response to the admonition that we must move fast or lose the opportunity: Our duty is to act with prudence and to do a risk/benefit analysis after a good-faith effort to research the facts. To paraphrase Francis Bacon, the slower man who keeps the right road accomplishes the mission faster than the fast runner who takes a wrong road in haste.

To deal with conflicts of interest, an area that requires special vigilance by board members, the American Bar Association stipulates three rules for nonprofit corporations: awareness, disclosure, and disinterested review. One has to be sensitive to possible conflicts and disclose the potential conflict to other board members so that those who are not involved in the potential conflict can do an objective review. The matter is decided by a vote of the board members not involved in the disclosed potential conflict.

The board member must not engage in activities that advance his or her interest at the expense of the organization.

Lessons Learned

- Learn basic accounting and investing analysis for service on a board.
- Understand clearly the fiduciary responsibilities of board members.
- Before introducing a proposal at a meeting, be prepared to present evidence that its advantages outweigh its risks. Also affirm that the proposal's purpose is relevant to the organization's mission.

CHAPTER 13

EXPANDING YOUR HORIZONS

Travel is fatal to prejudice, bigotry, and narrow-mindedness, and many of our people need it sorely on these accounts. Broad, wholesome, charitable views of men and things cannot be acquired by vegetating in one little corner of the earth all one's lifetime.

—Mark Twain

It was a long time ago. This is how I remember the tale.

There really was no alternative to the river and the crocodiles. The noise of the creatures advancing toward him was frightening because it signified death. The horde of marabunta ants would reach him in less than a minute as they devoured everything in their path. He imagined their giant pincers ripping him to shreds. He dove into the river and the crocodile watching him from the opposite shore slid into the water.

At that moment I heard the footsteps of the boarding school prefect as he walked between the rows of beds in the boarding school dormitory to ascertain that everyone was silent in the room and no lights remained on. The 9 p.m. "lights out" was strictly enforced and violators got demerits which could result in being "campused," a harsh penalty preventing you from leaving the grounds on Friday and Sunday nights—the only two nights one could leave the school boundary—with your grammar school classmates to walk a mile to the movie theater in town. I turned the flashlight off and closed the library book, *Bomba the Jungle Boy,* as my head emerged from under the covers hiding the light and the book.

That was a ritual I continued during my six years in boarding school. To me, Mark Twain's words about travel meant travel to faraway places with strange-sounding names. Of course, being sent to a boarding school at a young age was quite an adventure in itself. For a kid who had never left the Irish Channel neighborhood of New Orleans, the piney woods a mile outside of the town of Covington, Louisiana, were the closest thing to a jungle I had encountered. Here I learned how to distinguish poisonous snakes from nonpoisonous ones and how to capture both of them safely. This wasn't in the curriculum but it was dangerous adventure that appealed to kids. Those who failed to prepare by reading up on safety learned the lesson the hard way—by experience. I concluded that not doing the homework with the only source I had, books, was too risky. Remember, there was no TV or Internet. You learned from teachers, books, or experience.

I soon found out that there were fascinating creatures known as flying squirrels that lived in oak trees and came out at night. With long whiskers and the equivalent of a Batman cape attached to their front limbs, these small creatures glided from tree to tree. They made wonderful pets. I learned to trap one by attaching rubber bands to the hinged lid of a coffee can that would snap and close the opening when the lid was released. Then a hole was made in a pecan and a stick imbedded in the pecan with the other end of the stick holding the can lid open. When the squirrel tugged at the pecan, the lid snapped shut trapping the squirrel inside.

Unfortunately, the season to catch them was winter, when their food was scarce, and half of the squirrels died from the cold in the metal trap. When a wise teacher saw me looking sad at the death of a squirrel, he asked me if I could think of another material for the trap that reduced the cold hazard. His Socratic questioning led me to the workshop, where I built the first wooden trap used in that area. It looked like a shoebox. There were no further deaths when the trap was opened at dawn as I climbed the tree to check the trap before the 7 a.m. daily mass. All of this led to my interest in nature and science.

Reading, travel, and problem solving with innovation enrich a young life and give a broader perspective on challenges we all encounter later in life. My early experiences at boarding school certainly heightened my curiosity and led me to a lifetime of reading.

The library was small at the boarding school, and I finally read every book in it. The collection included the series of *Tarzan*, *The Hardy Boys*, and the tale of a British fighter pilot who did acrobatics as he fought Nazi fighter planes. He frequently said, "Cheerio, pip, pip, and all that sort of rot." I remember thinking the British speak English strangely. As an adult I remember telling a man from England that he had an accent. His response was, "You Americans have the accent!" Such encounters change one's perspective.

The library also introduced me to *Thirty Seconds Over Tokyo*, the heroic story of the Jimmie Doolittle Raid during World War II. These intrepid fliers bombed Japan in 1942 even though they realized they did not have enough fuel to return because of an unscheduled takeoff farther from Tokyo than had been planned when a Japanese patrol boat spotted their carrier, the USS *Hornet*.

Such adventures impress a child. I thought of the thrill of leaving the bounds of Earth and twisting in the wind in a plane. My mother showed me pictures of the two of us standing in front of my Dad's old biplane. All of these memories urged me to get into the sky. In the military, I learned to fly at an airbase aero club and went on to receive private and commercial licenses with an instrument rating. Soon after my discharge I bought a military T-34 aerobatic plane painted red, white, and blue and took aerobatic lessons. It had a sliding canopy with stars on the wings. On my days off, I took to the skies and did snap rolls, my only spectators being the alligators and nutria of the swamplands of eastern New Orleans.

Another important lesson I learned from the aerobatic experience was that I had to clear my mind of any pressing problem or I could not execute the maneuver properly. Such focus was refreshing and brought a different perspective when I returned to any difficult problem I had.

In 2004, at the invitation of Shanghai Mayor Sun Chao, I served on the International Advisory Board chaired by Professor Torsten N. Wiesel, former president of Rockefeller University and the winner of the 1981 Nobel Prize in Medicine for his work on vision. We went to a resort atop the Yellow Mountain (Mount Huangshan, in southeastern China) for a retreat to discuss an innovative massive medical center that was planned for the Xuhui District of Shanghai. While walking to the meeting room, I asked Professor Wiesel what environment he considered best for enabling creative thinking.

He said his best thoughts came to him while chopping wood, and that his focus was on the wood and nothing else. As he finished, suddenly an "Aha!" moment struck me: This is like flushing the RAM or transient memory of a computer and rebooting. Suddenly there is more space for additional thoughts. At least, that is the way I interpret Professor Wiesel's method.

"Reading maketh a full man; conference a ready man; and writing an exact man," Sir Francis Bacon said. Throughout history you will find advice that encourages reading. Most everyone has heard the thought that a person who does not read is no better off than the one who *cannot* read. Leaders read and learn. They observe and study to gain knowledge. This leads them to experience new adventures. They then reflect and gain insight to gain wisdom.

During one of my trips to China, a student asked me if I had heard of the novel *To Kill a Mockingbird*. I said yes, and he replied, "That is my favorite book." Once again, I saw the power of words. Words mean something. And at that moment across the world from my home, I realized that words can be loved and the message lived. Just imagine how stories now can be shared easily via the Internet. Freedom is on the march and censorship is impotent against the spread of ideas. As Victor Hugo, author of *Les Miserables*, said, "Nothing is more powerful than an idea whose time has come."

A lifetime of reading is essential for a leader. An explosion of knowledge and insight occurs at a rapid pace. A leader keeps up with the latest innovations and looks for opportunities to use those discoveries in his mission.

The seeds of leadership often are sown at a young age. One of the greatest gifts a parent can give a child is the love of reading.

Reading also introduces stirring oratory to the emerging leader. You can learn from the past not only what happened, but also how leaders organized the facts into a persuasive argument to convince others to agree or follow.

Read *The American Crisis*, written by Thomas Paine when the Americans were in retreat from the British attack at Fort Lee, and you'll realize what effect logic and eloquence can have on dispirited troops. George Washington had it read to his men. It begins:

These are the times that try men's souls. The summer soldier and the sunshine patriot will, in this crisis, shrink from the service of his country; but he that stands it now, deserves the love and thanks of man and woman.

Tyranny, like hell, is not easily conquered; yet we have this consolation with us, that the harder the conflict, the more glorious the triumph. What we obtain too cheap, we esteem too lightly; 'Tis dearness only that gives everything its value. Heaven knows how to put a proper price upon its goods; and it would be strange indeed if so celestial an article as Freedom should not be highly rated.[1]

It was Paine's eloquence expressed in passionate, simple words that was an elixir for the fledgling nation. As Donald T. Phillips points out in *The Founding Fathers on Leadership*, "[Paine] inspired others to act—for certain shared goals that represent the wants and needs, the aspirations and expectations—of the people."[2]

Leaders recognize the importance of writing down pithy quotes for later use. I advise carrying an electronic device such as a PDA that allows you to type in the quote or write on the screen. Be sure to back it up on your computer as soon as possible in the event you lose the PDA or the memory gets erased going through a security checkpoint at an airport.

In debates or discussions, you can refer to these gems to make a point. Leaders realize the importance of analogies and storytelling. Consider a few from the thousands I have collected.

"It is a socialist idea that making profits is a vice. I consider the real vice is making losses."

—Winston Churchill

- [Take a moment from the stress of each day and reflect on ways to create new wealth and enrich yourself and the world. DJP]

"Those who love deeply never grow old; they may die of old age, but they die young."

—Sir Arthur Wing Pinero

"The real price of everything is the toil and trouble of acquiring it."

—Adam Smith

"A man that seeks truth and loves it must be reckoned precious to any human society."

—Frederick the Great

"Whenever you commend, add your reasons for doing so; it is this which distinguishes the approbation of a man of sense from the flattery of sycophants and admiration of fools."

—Richard Steele

"To give real service you must add something which cannot be bought or measured with money, and that is sincerity and integrity."

—Donald A. Adams

"To live in the presence of great truths and eternal laws, to be led by permanent ideals—that is what keeps a man patient when the world ignores him, and calm and unspoiled when the world praises him."

—Honoré de Balzac

"When an archer misses the mark he turns and looks for the fault within himself. Failure to hit the bull's-eye is never the fault of the target. To improve your aim, improve yourself."

—Gilbert Arland

• [Also, I have noted that when faced with a problem, it is more productive to search for solutions rather than blame. DJP]

"A stumble may prevent a fall."

—Thomas Fuller

• [Do not lament too long when you stumble; reflect, learn, correct, and move on to success. DJP]

"I am certain of nothing but the holiness of the heart's affections and the truth of imagination."

—John Keats

• [Take time to love and imagine. DJP]

And don't forget poetry, plays, and essays. A good starting place for essays is *50 Great Essays*, edited by Houston Peterson.[3] In that collection you can read selected works of Montaigne, Bacon, Swift, Lamb, Thoreau, E. B. White, and many more. Also include in your study published trial summation speeches to the jury or judges such as the July 26, 1946, closing argument at Nuremberg, Germany, of Robert H. Jackson, chief counsel for the United States in the war crimes trial of Nazi officials.[4] It gives a powerful lesson in presenting facts in a compelling way that leads to only one conclusion.

All potential leaders should do their best to read, travel, and learn. Curiosity is important for all of us. More important are the lessons learned and actions taken.

Finally, it is important to get the maximum use out of the body your genes gave you. If you won a Lamborghini or Corvette Z06 sports car, you certainly would not pour sand or dirt into the oil or the fuel injectors. Yet that is what many people do with something that is more valuable than an exotic sports car: their bodies. They don't exercise, they don't maintain a normal weight, they eat junk food, and they smoke. Of all the dangerous habits, smoking has to be among the worst. Smoking causes lung cancer and can create ulcers in the arteries that bring blood to the brain, with resulting emboli and stroke.

Keep in mind that weight gain is influenced greatly by two factors: calories ingested and calories burned. Eating gives the calories. Exercise burns the calories. For every 3,500 calories that you ingest over the amount you need to maintain your weight, you gain one pound. So if you eat more, you have to exercise more. Try walking at least five days a week. Get checked out by your physician if you have medical problems and need a custom program of exercise.

And one more thing. Don't be discouraged from traveling or reading by negative people. Negative people don't advance your interests. There is nothing wrong with constructive criticism. In fact, then Dean Donald Jacobs of the Kellogg School of Management taught me that you should hug people who bring you "disconfirming opinions." Sometimes the criticisms can teach you and allow you to change course. But I am now referring to the people who are always negative. Why waste a moment of your life listening to them? Time waits for no one, and, as my surgical partner for over thirty years, Dr. Jim Brown, says, "We are here by a thread; at any time it may snap." Treasure your time and use it wisely.

Lessons Learned

- One of the greatest gifts a parent can give a child is the love of reading. The seeds of leadership often are sown at a young age.
- A lifetime of reading is important.
- Learn from the past and get inspired.
- Write down pithy quotes for later use.
- Memorize quotes from poems.
- Travel broadens one's perspective and allows you to experience different cultures and appreciate what you have at home.

- Travel makes you a more interesting conversationalist.
- Observe and study to gain knowledge.
- Do not resist new adventures.
- Reflect and gain insight to gain wisdom.
- Eat healthful foods and exercise.
- Don't let others discourage you from reading and travel.
- A leader is not a narrow-minded person.

CHAPTER 14

PUTTING INFORMATION TECHNOLOGY TO USE

Doing research on the Web is like using a library assembled piecemeal by packrats and vandalized nightly.[1]

—Roger Ebert

In 1994 I was a candidate for the American Medical Association's Board of Trustees. I had never served on one of the AMA councils, and doing that was a stepping-stone toward becoming a trustee. Frequently, members served on various councils for eight or nine years and then tossed their hats into the ring for a board position. The Louisiana State Medical Society (LSMS) approved my entry in the race, which was an important prerequisite, as the chances of winning were nonexistent without your own state society's approval.

However, some long-time observers of AMA politics said the chances of my winning were slim to none, and it was a waste of the state society's time and money. Whenever a candidate from Louisiana was in an election, among the expected expenses was a "Louisiana Gumbo Party." Money also was needed for any brochures or lapel pins. I believed we could win the confidence of the voters from all over the nation in the AMA house of delegates by giving them information about my experience in Louisiana and on the debate circuit.

Once I entered the race for a trustee position, I had a communication advantage. It was a newsletter that the LSMS had tested in 1987 in a successful campaign for a colleague from Louisiana who ran for vice speaker of the AMA's house of delegates. The newsletter, *The Pelican*, was sent out every several months during the year prior to the trustee election. It was sent to the AMA delegates and then produced daily by LSMS at the house of delegates annual meeting held in a Chicago hotel, adding information from the activities of the previous day in the house of delegates.

I have been taking photographs since I was sixteen and continued doing so during my time at the AMA.

I took pictures of delegates at meetings and frequently captured them on film or digital media when they were testifying at the microphone. Those photos ended up in some issues of *The Pelican*. That was one feature motivating people to read the newsletter, in addition to getting the recipe for some famous dish served at a great New Orleans restaurant. Finally, they could read my columns, containing my views on a variety of subjects. (See examples of *The Pelican* for the years 1996–2002 at http://www.intrepidresources. com/html/pelican_newsletters.html and don't forget to check out the recipes!)

I lost a close race in 1994, but I ran again in 1996 using the same technique and won on the first ballot. Without the use of photography and other forms of technology, I doubt that I would have had enough exposure to the delegates to get elected. Of course, an important lesson advertising man David Ogilvy taught in his books was that advertising doesn't make you successful; you have to have a worthwhile product. A poor product disappears from the marketplace faster with advertising. More people try it and spread the word that it is not a good product.

The opposite occurs with advertising and a good product. He also said, "In the modern world of business, it is useless to be a creative, original thinker unless you can also sell what you create."

But there are important advantages of using information technology other than advertising.

Remember, information technology is a tool. It alone is not sufficient for an emerging leader.

In addition to the essential elements of leadership already discussed, one has to have help from trusted individuals. Let me give you one example. When I ran for the AMA board of trustees, the single most important decision I made was asking Dr. W. Juan Watkins to be my campaign manager. He is a respected and extremely organized physician from Shreveport, Louisiana, who had years of experience on the budget and finance committee of the Louisiana State Medical Society. On this committee he excelled in organizing and budgeting. He made it simple for me to go to the eighteen interviews with the various AMA state and specialty delegations over several days prior to the election.

Dr. Watkins went to Chicago, where the election was going to be held, a few weeks before the convention and looked up all of the scattered interview sites in the hotel as well as outside the hotel. No one asked him to do this or even thought of it. It was his idea and demonstrated his leadership abilities. He timed the walking distance or cab distance to each site. At each interview site, I was given anywhere from two to ten minutes to speak and then there was a question and answer session. As soon as the interview was over, I had to be at the next interview site, sometimes within ten minutes. As a candidate, you want to focus on your message, reflect on how you might have made a previous answer clearer, and avoid the anxiety of being unable to find the next interview location, thereby taking the opportunity to meet with that caucus. Dr. Watkins eliminated that stress. Several times I saw other candidates in a panic because they did not know how to find the next interview location. Dr. Watkins always helped them.

I consider several gadgets extremely helpful for an emerging leader. Essential is a laptop computer with wireless access to the Internet, and then additional devices that either perform one function or a number of functions—taking photos, receiving e-mail, storing notes, and making and receiving phone calls. I like the idea of separate devices because if the combination device is lost or malfunctions, you don't lose all capability. If you lose the phone, you can communicate by e-mail with the PDA. A PDA has a calendar scheduler, can send and receive e-mail, store photos, and notes and more. Some even play music. Newer models take photos and download music from the Internet. One can think of a PDA as a palm-sized computer that serves as a substitute for the laptop or desktop computer when you do not have access to them.

One bonus gadget for leaders is a portable Global Positioning Satellite (GPS) device, which pinpoints on a small screen your geographic location, with the exact latitude and longitude. Either as a separate item or as part of your portable phone, a GPS device can be invaluable in many situations. In a disaster, while traveling, or whenever a rescue is needed, a GPS device can save valuable time and even lives. I use one worldwide and, with the portable handheld stand-alone unit I use, there is no charge for readings from satellites. With my backup GPS system on my portable phone, there is a monthly fee for the GPS service.

The usefulness of the camera is not limited to photographing people and scenery. Saving paper documents for years and retrieving them quickly can be a burden. But it is simple with a digital camera. Digital images are exceptionally easy to store and retrieve on computer disks, allowing you to take pictures of documents or interesting news articles and then discard the paper. Identifying each image is similarly easy. Often, there is no need to label each image. Just put the new series of images in a folder with the name of the topic and add the date the photo was taken or the date on the article. Modern computer search engines can find the folder in seconds.

I use a PDA for storing important documents or clippings of articles. It is readily accessible in meetings and eliminates the problem of a person forgetting where an important article is stored. Is it at the office? Is it at home? Was it discarded? A person may not remember that the document was saved. This method of electronic storage allows immediate access and confirms the exact wording of the position paper, press release, or other document. If you can't recall if you stored it in the PDA, an electronic search will yield the answer in seconds.

Of course, one has to retain backup copies of all digital files. I recommend that you back up at home or the office and have another backup in a distant location that will be safe from any fire, flood, or other disaster that might destroy the original. This can be done with external hard drives or other storage devices such as compact discs, or USB flash drives. You can keep a spare copy of the backup near the computer and the other backup copy in a distant secure location. Finally you can keep backups at an online storage site.

When writing this book, I took the precaution to backup every chapter on two external hard drives plus two USB flash drives. One of the flash drives was kept on my key ring. I also printed out each chapter to have a hard copy in my possession. On a recent lecture trip, I was asked at airport security to step aside for additional checking because of the gadgets and chargers in my carry-on luggage. After the magnetic-wand scan, I discovered that the data in my personal digital assistant was erased! However, the data was backed up in my laptop computer, and in minutes all of the data was restored in my PDA. Watch out for magnets! And don't forget to back up data.

You also need to look ahead and be certain that your stored backup information can be retrieved in the future. As technology advances, different connectors and data-reading devices change. You must anticipate this and keep some older equipment that will read the data or upgrade to the new technology while the opportunity exists to transfer from old equipment to new. A USB or Firewire connector may not be included in the computers of the future. There may be some quantum leap device that doesn't access the previous connectors or tapes or discs.

To best use technology, you must select equipment that makes it easy for you to store information and retrieve it quickly and easily. Search engines that label every word as a keyword make searching easy with large collections of data.

The amount of digital data available is increasing dramatically, making it harder to locate what you need. In 2003 Verlyn Klinkenborg wrote in *The New York Times* that a study at the University of California at Berkley "estimated that in 2002 the human species stored about five exabytes of new information on paper, film, optical or magnetic media, a number that doubled in the past three years. Five exabytes, as it happens, is equivalent to all words ever spoken by humans since the dawn of time."[2]

My laptop computer has a one-hundred gigabyte hard drive. As a refresher, there are about 250 words on a page and that equals two kilobytes of data. A kilobyte is 1,000 bytes or ten to the third power (actually 1,024 bytes because electronic memory circuits correctly are identified in binary numbers, so it is two to the tenth power) and a gigabyte is one billion bytes (ten to the sixth power). An exabyte is one quintillion bytes (ten to the eighteenth power). Thus five exabytes would equal the storage space of fifty billion notebook computers like mine.[3]

The amount of stored electronic data obviously will increase as the years go by. Bob DeCoufle wrote in *The Data Center Journal* that according to a report from IDC (International Data Corporation, an information technology company), the world generated 161 billion gigabytes—161 exabytes—of digital information last year. That's like twelve stacks of books that each reach from the earth to the sun. Or you might think of it as three million times the information in all the books ever written, according to IDC.[4,5]

Obviously, information overload is here. The advantage of learning how to search the vast data warehouse of information with easy-to-use gadgets is obvious. In addition, articles, recordings, and photos that will be of value to you in future research can be stored on portable devices for quick retrieval without the need to access the Internet. The postage-stamp sized memory cards that can be inserted into PDAs make it possible to carry vast amounts of information with you in very small devices.

Find gadgets that you consider easy to use and reliable. There is always someone with a love of technology willing to give candid advice to a novice. Once hooked on the usefulness of these devices, you never will go back to the old ways of recording research and other documents on paper. Soon you will marvel at the creativity of the inventors of these wonderful devices.

I once showed my father a new gadget I bought. He smiled and said, "Son, didn't I buy you enough toys when you were a kid?" If you have a love of technology, an added bonus is the enhanced connection with the grandkids because they were born in the digital age.

Lessons Learned

- Portable technology gadgets and information retrieval are important tools for the emerging leader.
- Having critical information but not being able to retrieve it timely is no better than not having the information at all.
- Be creative in using cameras not only for portraits but also as storage devices for newspaper articles and documents.

- Backing up data is critical, and additional backup in another location gives important protection in the event of flood, fire, or other disaster.
- Avoid exposing digital devices to magnetic equipment to prevent data erasure.

CHAPTER 15

BULLIES, AN IMPEDIMENT TO LEADERSHIP

All cruelty springs from weakness.

—Lucius Annaeus Seneca, 4 BCE–CE 65

It was the usual hot New Orleans summer. The youngster picked up the basketball in the deserted schoolyard. Although he never was an outstanding ballplayer in his grammar school class, it always felt good to dribble the ball and imagine he was making baskets from all over the court. Besides, it felt good to be out of the house. This was the first time since his hernia surgery the week before.

Suddenly he realized that two older kids were approaching him quickly.

"Hi, what's up?" he said.

"We were looking for a little kid to beat up and we picked you."

In a flash, the younger boy thought that outrunning them would be impossible, but there was a chance he'd find other people on the street who might intervene. He dropped the basketball and started running, paying no attention to the doctor's admonition not to run for six weeks after the operation. He was surprised at the burst of energy that kept him ahead of the pursuers. He ran into an alley that led to his house, but the gate at the end of it was locked.

Now he was trapped in the alley.

The bullies approached with what looked to the kid like evil grins as they tightened their fists. Now he knew what fear was. Now it was real, not just something he had read about in comic books, where, if the bad guys outnumbered the good guys, the superhero always arrived just in time to save the day.

From out of nowhere, somebody said in a loud voice, "What's going on here?"

It was enough to make the boy believe in guardian angels. The voice was unmistakably his father's.

The other kids froze.

"Dad," the kid blurted out, "they're going to beat me up!"

"Well, it doesn't look like a fair fight to me, two big kids against one small one," his father said in a calm, steady voice. "Son, pick up that broken broomstick by your feet."

The kid quickly picked up the broomstick.

What the boy saw next remained with him for the rest of his life: The two older kids turned and ran. It was a real-life demonstration that they were bullies and that bullies are cowards. I was that young boy and the observation that bullies are cowards was imprinted on my brain as deeply as any school lesson ever was.

A bully is someone who can threaten, tease, or hurt someone the bully perceives as weaker. At the heart of this behavior is low self-esteem. Even though the bully is a coward, it does not mean the bully is not dangerous. As a general rule, the bully will not engage in a fair fight or one where the bully is not guaranteed of winning.

Ignoring a bully is good advice. But when the bully corners a person, the person should not go without a fight into the victim role. As Benjamin Disraeli said, "Courage is fire, and bullying is smoke."

Leaders identify bullies and have zero tolerance for them. The victims of bullies sometimes snap and become predators who punish all they perceive as perpetrators or enablers. That is why prevention programs and early identification programs with accountability are important for schools.

Individuals who aspire to be leaders must realize they cannot stand idly by when bullies are in action.

Failure to speak out causes others not to trust them in a leadership position. Leaders must have courage and integrity. They must earn trust.

Movies and stories that show individuals standing up to bullies always elicit positive audience response. Just look at *Shane* (six Academy Award Nominations), *High Noon* (five Academy Awards and three additional nominations), *From Here to Eternity* (eight Academy Awards and five additional nominations), and *And Justice for All* (two Academy Award nominations). Even Charlie Brown of "Peanuts" fame plays the hero as he goes up against the camp bully with the aid of Joe Cool (aka Snoopy) in *He's a Bully, Charlie Brown*.

Lessons Learned

- Bullies are cowards who have low self-esteem.
- Expose bullies and get help.
- Don't remain silent when observing bullies attacking someone else.
- Bullies can prevent leadership from emerging if courage is not shown.

CHAPTER 16

SOME LEADERS YOU MAY NEVER HAVE HEARD OF (AND SOME YOU HAVE)

Management is doing things right; leadership is doing the right things.

—Peter F. Drucker

In 1991, near Fort Campbell, Kentucky, a military training exercise with live ammunition was in progress. A soldier tripped and accidentally fired his M-16 rifle.

The bullet struck the battalion commander, a lieutenant colonel who had been first in his class at the U.S. Army Ranger School. It entered the officer's chest just above his name tag and exited at his back, leaving a large gaping wound. He fell to the ground and remained conscious. A general standing next to him administered first aid and called for a medical evacuation helicopter.

The officer was flown to Vanderbilt Medical Center in Nashville, Tennessee. The accidental shooting occurred on a Saturday, so the general called ahead to be sure the best surgeon was available.

The surgeon met the helicopter and saved the man's life after five hours of surgery. The surgeon was Dr. William "Bill" Frist, who later became the Republican Senate majority leader. And who was the wounded soldier? The same person who received an 81–0 vote of confirmation in January 2007 to lead U.S. and multinational forces in Iraq—four-star General David Petraeus.

I told that story in April 2007 during a speech at the Tennessee Medical Association ceremony honoring, Dr. Frist in Nashville. After my speech, Dr. Frist asked how I came to know the story about him and Petraeus. I told him that, in preparing for my speech, I found the information while poring through an almost endless list of Web sites that contained his name. The fact that the story never received extensive publicity demonstrates that Dr. Frist never used it to further his career. This kind of humility is a hallmark of leaders. Both General Petraeus and Dr. Frist are competent professionals who excel in any arena they enter. Dr. Frist's relentless pursuit of excellence in medicine gave him the skills for that lifesaving operation. He also performed the first successful combined heart-lung transplant in the southeastern United States. Both of the individuals in this story are leaders in the thick of action. They do not put others at risk while they direct from afar.

Dr. Frist was a leader in promoting the Patient Safety and Quality Improvement Act of 2005. Among the other Senate accomplishments I mentioned about Dr. Frist in my speech was his strong advocacy of reforming medical liability.

Dr. Frist and President George W. Bush led this fight in Congress. Repeatedly, Dr. Frist brought commonsense legislation on the issue to a vote in the Senate after it had passed the House of Representatives. Although he had the majority of votes for passage in the Senate, it was not possible to overcome a filibuster because cloture required sixty senators to bring the legislation to the Senate floor for a debate and a vote on its merits. However, the resulting publicity spurred successful legislation at the state level in several crisis states, notably Texas, where the medical liability rates immediately decreased dramatically and the physician licensing board had to hire more staff to process the applications of the many physicians who moved to Texas because of that legislation.

Snapshots of Other Leaders

I examine leaders in other chapters, but I include other deserving ones here to honor them and emphasize that leadership is not limited to any one field or walk of life.

Dr. Zhu Chen, China's Minister of Health

In 2007 I was selected by Health Minister Zhu Chen to give a keynote address at the Fifth Sino-U.S. Symposium on "Medicine in the 21st Century," in Shanghai. My topic was "Ethics and Law in Medical Discovery, Clinical Trials, and Digital Health Records."

Dr. Zhu Chen was the first noncommunist to become health minister in the People's Republic of China since the Communist Party came to power in 1949. His official biography at his inauguration into the prestigious National Academy of Sciences in the U.S., written by David Bradley, states, in part, that

> Chen has been the principal figure behind the development of a radical approach to acute promyelocytic leukemia (APL) that combines the arsenic of traditional Chinese medicine (TCM) with Western medicine. His work in this area has provided a molecular rationale for an effective cancer therapy. It led to his election to the National Academy of Sciences in 2003.

The alchemist's symbol for arsenic is a menacing coiled serpent, and perhaps rightly so. The element of arsenic has certainly earned a great deal of infamy from the reign of the Borgias to the novels of Agatha Christie, and in more recent times as a toxic contaminant of drinking water. But the symbolic serpent also coils around the staff of Aesculapius, an international symbol for medicine; arsenic the poison is also arsenic the healer.

His path to medicine and discovery was not easy. Bradley continues

Chen left academia at an early age. "I left primary school in Shanghai in 1966," he said. "The so-called Cultural Revolution had begun, and, like most of my contemporaries, I went to work in the countryside and lost the opportunity to pursue studies in middle school and university."[1]

However with self-study and his noted work as a "barefoot doctor," the term given to farmers who were given basic first-aid medical and public health training, he eventually was able to go to college and medical school. He subsequently studied in France, where he received his Ph.D. In 1989, he left France and began work on the APL form of leukemia at the Shanghai Institute of Hematology at Rui Jin Hospital.

At dinner with Dr. Zhu Chen the night before I delivered my keynote address, my wife Robin asked Dr. Zhu Chen how his discovery occurred. He stated that arsenic could help people who relapsed from conventional therapy and the idea occurred to him and his colleagues, "Why don't we use this at the beginning rather than waiting for them to relapse? When we put the two things together the miracle occurred." He gave a big smile and continued; "Now we have a five-year survival rate of ninety-four percent." He praised the work of his colleagues at the Shanghai Institute of Hematology and said it was a team effort that led to this breakthrough.

On my visit to Shanghai in 2004 to speak at and co-moderate the Third Sino-American Symposium and again in 2007, Dr. Zhu Chen impressed me as someone with the attributes I listed for leadership. What is immediately obvious when visiting with him is his gentle nature, kindness, and humility.

Dr. James P. Bagian, NASA Astronaut

Dr. James Bagian is a mulitalented leader—an engineer, physician, pilot, and astronaut. After the 1986 *Challenger* space shuttle explosion, he supervised the capsule's recovery from the ocean floor, personally diving ninety-five feet into the Atlantic Ocean and discovering the bodies. He served on the team that investigated the tragedy. Dr. Bagian also was one of the investigators following the *Columbia* space shuttle's disintegration disaster that occurred in 2003 upon re-entry into the earth's atmosphere.

He led efforts to develop a pressure suit used for shuttle crew escape, a shuttle escape hatch, and other related survival equipment. He also designed a new ejection seat for military aircraft to minimize injuries on ejection.

He was the first person to successfully treat space motion sickness. NASA adopted his treatment as the standard of care for the control of this illness in shuttle crews and it continues to be routinely used. As a crewmember of two space shuttle missions, he logged more than 347 hours in space.

Dr. Bagian is the director of the Veterans Health Administration's National Center for Patient Safety. I have observed him during meetings of the board of governors of the National Patient Safety Foundation. When Dr. Bagian speaks, people listen.

This is what Dr. Bagian told me about leadership when I interviewed him in December of 2007:

Leadership is about identifying where you want to go, why it is important to go, and what's in it for others—both the positive and the negative. Leaders lead by example. Leadership is personal. It is working shoulder to shoulder. You must show you are willing to get your hands dirty. You must work at least as hard as those you wish to lead. They eat first.

They get sleeping quarters first. You will put yourself at risk, both professionally and physically. Leadership is service before self. Just as Ben Franklin said, "Do well by doing good."[2]

Bobby Jindal, Governor of Louisiana

Former U.S. Rep. Bobby Jindal of Louisiana is the first person of Indian-American heritage in the United States to be elected governor of a state. A former Rhodes Scholar, he was inaugurated as governor of Louisiana on January 14, 2008, in Baton Rouge where he was born thirty-six years ago. His election was widely considered a watershed event in the history of Louisiana, thanks to a campaign that was sharply focused on establishing ethical standards and ending the state's long history of corruption and scandal, and its deeply embedded patronage system. Ethics reform tops the list of Jindal's agenda. The day before his inauguration, he told the press, "We are going to start with the war on corruption." Keep your eyes on Louisiana as future historians may say 2008 was the start of the renaissance of Louisiana.

I have known Bobby Jindal since he was twenty-one years old and followed his career closely. He has superior intelligence, does his homework, listens carefully to views of others, speaks without equivocation, and is a visionary. His kindness and graciousness are widely recognized. It will not surprise me to see him as a popular candidate for president of the United States in the years ahead.

When I asked Governor Jindal for his definition of leadership he told me that "a leader has to be brave enough to stick to his principles while being decisive, able to build a coalition based on consensus, possess the vision to guide his people and see beyond short-term obstacles, and be willing to sacrifice his own interests to serve others."[3]

Dr. Richard Anderson

I serve on the board of The Doctors Company (TDC) in Napa, California and have the opportunity to work with a brilliant leader who is the company's chairman and chief executive officer.

I first met Dr. Anderson in 2003, when we were sitting on a three-member panel at a hearing of the National Association of Insurance Commissioners on insurance-market conditions and reform of the medical malpractice system. The third panel member was a plaintiff's attorney. After that meeting I knew I had met an intelligent man in Dr. Anderson, as he was efficient in debate and full of facts. He gets the big picture and doesn't miss the forest because of focusing on one tree. He became the person I wanted to have at my side in any battle for medical liability reform.

In addition to his writings, speeches, and leadership of the largest physician-owned medical liability company, he demonstrates qualities that an ideal leader should have. He is courageous in debate, is respectful to others, listens carefully, and doesn't have hidden agendas about the plans for the organization. He is not a power-hungry leader who wants to withhold information and use the excuse that it has to be his way because "you don't know all of the facts and I can't tell them to you."

In January of 2008, I asked Dr. Anderson to give me his definition of leadership. His response was:

> Here is what true leadership is:
> Not inherited.
> Not assumed.
> Not seized.
> Not maintained by force.
> Not strengthened by the ignorance of the led.
> Not based on coercion any more than a prison guard should be said to be a leader of prisoners.

Then he added,

> True leadership is not based on superior power, but on superior vision.
> A true leader is someone who others willingly follow. The stronger, more independent, more thoughtful, more competent, more accomplished the followers, the better the leader must be, and will be.

There is no true leadership in which the leader wins and the followers lose.[4]

Philip Howard

Philip Howard is one of the leading advocates of legal reform in the nation. A prominent lawyer and best-selling author, he is changing the way America thinks about the impact that lawsuits and the regulatory maze have on our lives.

His first book, *The Death of Common Sense: How Law is Suffocating America,* became an immediate best seller when it was published in 1995. It chronicles the many ways in which commonsense actions have been stifled by a regulatory philosophy that leaves no room for human judgment.

His following book, *The Collapse of the Common Good: How America's Lawsuit Culture Undermines Our Freedom,* has spawned a national movement. It focuses on the fear instilled by the ability of any one to sue over almost anything and the paralyzing impact this has on our common institutions such as health care and education.

The national movement, which Howard founded and chairs, is called Common Good. Its purpose is to reform our lawsuit culture, and it has generated broad bipartisan support. Its board, for example, includes both George McGovern and Newt Gingrich.

After graduating from Yale University and the University of Virginia Law School, Howard began practicing law in New York City. There he founded his own law firm, Howard, Darby & Levin, which later merged with a leading Washington, D.C., firm, Covington & Burling, of which he is now vice chairman.

In recognition of his untiring efforts to bring common sense to the legal system, he received the American Medical Association's Presidential Citation on March 29, 2004, at the annual President's Forum in Washington during my tenure as president of the AMA.

Howard has accepted many leadership roles, including fighting to protect Central Park from the effects of proposed commercial development nearby. *The Village Voice* named him one of "New York's Heroes." In addition to being vice chairman of the law firm of Covington & Burling, he continues to be a prominent civic leader in New York. Howard chairs the Municipal Art Society and chaired the committee that installed the "Tribute in Light" memorial for those lost in the World Trade Center terrorist attack.

It was very exciting to share the podium with Howard and Dr. Richard Anderson at the U.S. Chamber of Commerce 2003 Legal Reform Summit. Those are teammates I will go with into any debate. It truly was an exciting day. Here is an except from one of Howard's articles:

American justice has become a parody of itself. This week's example is the $54 million lawsuit by a lawyer in Washington, D.C., against his dry cleaners for losing a pair of pants. Now the tort reform debate—tired sloganeering about "frivolous lawsuits" versus "the right to sue"—has come to the point of self-parody as well. Robert Bork, long-time critic of "the litigation lottery," has sued the Yale Club for "in excess of $1,000,000" as a result of a fall he took while trying to step onto the dais to make a speech last year.[5]

The Leaders of Hurricane Katrina

Although this chapter could encompass an entire book, I wish to cite a few examples of exceptional leadership during the aftermath of Hurricane Katrina.

General Russel Honoré's actions in New Orleans brought order to chaos after Hurricane Katrina. He retired from the Army in 2007 but I predict we have not heard the last of him.

Many doctors in New Orleans who volunteered to stay during Hurricane Katrina and help others despite horrible conditions in the aftermath of the Hurricane. These include:

Dr. Brobson Lutz, featured in a front-page story in the *Wall Street Journal*, who set up a clinic in the French Quarter after Katrina and helped remove the dead when no one else would do it.

Dr. Jim Aiken at Charity Hospital, featured on CNN as one of the "Angels of Katrina," and Dr. Norman McSwain at Tulane, featured in *The New York Times* for his medical care to patients in the hurricane-damaged Tulane University Hospital & Clinic.

Dr. Jan McClanahan at Methodist Hospital in eastern New Orleans, a surgical partner of mine for more than thirty years, who operated during Hurricane Katrina by flashlight and stayed there until the last helicopter rescuing those trapped at the hospital left.

Then there are the three doctors who did heroic work at the city's Memorial Hospital during the most publicized episode in New Orleans in the aftermath of Hurricane Katrina. Those three are Drs. Richard Deichmann, John Walsh, Jr., and Anna Pou. To get an insider's view of what it was like for the 2,000 people trapped inside the flooded hospital with temperatures more than one hundred degrees, dead bodies, and sewage overflowing from toilets, read Dr. Deichmann's book, *Code Blue: A Katrina Physician's Memoir Post-Katrina.*[6]

Dr. Karen DeSalvo, chief of general medicine and geriatrics at Tulane, continues to show great leadership with her work setting up clinics for those who have no access to doctors after Hurricane Katrina.

Two groups must be mentioned. The "women of the storm," founded by Anne Milling, did outstanding grassroots work lobbying in Congress educating legislators about the aftermath of Hurricanes Katrina and Rita, Citizens for 1 Greater New Orleans, Chaired by Ruthie Frierson, did important education and lobbying of Louisiana legislators regarding consolidation of levee boards and assessors as well as giving transparency to the criminal justice system and more.

Mayor Rudolph Giuliani

And let me mention the man who is known for his work as mayor of New York, my wife's favorite city. Rudolph Giuliani's actions after the horrific terrorist attack on September 11, 2001, led to his being named "America's mayor." He showed strong leadership in that tragedy and the compliments were well deserved. However, I also see him as a leader who took New York from a nearly bankrupt city full of crime to a place that thrives and prospers. Others may say that many had planned all of this, but Mayor Giuliani made it happen.

Dr. Robert D. Sparks

Dr. Robert Sparks is a quiet leader who is a model of civility. I have known him since his days as dean of the Tulane University School of Medicine from 1969 to 1972, when he was the second youngest medical school dean in the United States. He went on to many other important positions, including chancellor of the University of Nebraska Medical Center, vice president of the University of Nebraska, and president and chief programming officer of the W. K. Kellogg Foundation.

While at the Kellogg Foundation, Sparks was a pioneer in the development of leadership training. On the fiftieth anniversary of the foundation, created in 1930, Sparks led the effort to establish the Kellogg National Fellowship Program, a leadership development program that later became international as well. The KNFP launched a study of leadership in the United States that continues today.

On a personal note: In 1967 and 1968 I was chief resident of surgery at Tulane and on a rotation to a charity hospital outside of New Orleans. I noted the hospital's lack of an external defibrillator. I asked the hospital administrator to buy one. He refused. I met with Dean Sparks at Tulane and explained to him the need for this critical piece of equipment. The dean agreed and wrote a supporting letter strongly urging the purchase of a defibrillator. The administrator still refused and said he planned to use the money to buy a photocopier.

A couple of months later the administrator was admitted to the internal medical service of the hospital with a chest complaint. I was making rounds on the patient ward with a visiting professor of surgery and the junior residents and medical students. Out came the administrator into the hall where we were talking. He clutched his chest and fell to the floor. He was unresponsive. We immediately began cardiopulmonary resuscitation. The EKG showed fibrillation of his heart. He opened his eyes and looked at us as we gave him oxygen via the endotracheal tube. Because we had no external defibrillator, we had to carry him to the operating room, continuing resuscitation en route, open his chest and attempt defibrillation with the internal paddles directly to the heart. Unfortunately, he died.

Dr. Edward Annis

Dr. Edward Annis is a legend at the American Medical Association and to physicians nationwide. He is widely considered the person who correctly predicted the results of government controlled medical care. In 1962 he met with President Kennedy and pointed out the flaws in a proposed government controlled healthcare system. He predicted interference with the patient-physician relationship, rationing, and government control of the physician's medical judgment. For more details of his outstanding work, read his book, *Code Blue: Health Care in Crisis*.[7]

In November 2007 I took a walk with Dr. Annis, who was then ninety-four years old, and spoke with him on the subject of leadership. His mind remained sharp and he was as impressive at ninety-four as when he was a young surgeon on the media tours as

AMA president talking about government interference with the practice of medicine. After our conversation, he later wrote me with additional thoughts.

For those who aspire to be leaders, Dr. Annis says that, "important factors in delivering good speeches are preparation and knowledge of both your subject and the group you'll be addressing. Be honest, be straightforward. Think in terms of words and phrases that people can understand. It is important for leaders to be sufficiently well prepared to allow them; to focus attention on the people they are talking to."[8]

His other recommendations were to: be on time for any called meeting; be truthful always; be tolerant and make room for those who hold different opinions; have common sense; be aware that everybody makes mistakes now and then, and when you know your cause is just, never give up.

Ron Faucheux

Ron Faucheux is a former state legislator—from my home state of Louisiana—where he defeated an incumbent to become the legislature's youngest member at the tender age of twenty-five. He's also a political media consultant who has handled more than 116 candidate and issue campaigns in eleven states.

He is publisher emeritus and contributor at large of *Campaigns and Elections* magazine, a nonpartisan publication that provides an insider's view of politics.

He also produces the Political Oddsmaker, an online elections handicapping service.

Faucheux has a unique background that combines experience as a candidate, public official, journalist, political analyst, and campaign consultant. He's written numerous articles and has served as an analyst, commentator, and research source for news organizations worldwide.

Faucheux received a B.S. degree from Georgetown University's School of Foreign Service, a Ph.D. in political science from the University of New Orleans, and a Juris Doctor degree from LSU Law School. He teaches in the Graduate School of Political Management at George Washington University.

About leadership, he says that, "the components of leadership—be it political, professional, civic, religious, or military—include the clarity of vision to know where you want to go; the ability to understand and communicate the wants and needs of potential followers; the credibility to inspire trust in those followers; the determination to persevere when things get difficult; the skill to identify and remove obstacles along the way; and the wisdom to know when you, in fact, have arrived at your ultimate destination."[9]

Dr. Henry Giles

Dr. Henry Giles received his medical degree from Tulane in 1962. He completed his internship at Tulane and Charity Hospital in New Orleans and was drafted into the Army. Because he eventually would be doing medical rescue work in the hostile environment of a fight zone during the Vietnam War, Giles received survival and weapons training from the Green Berets.

In Vietnam with the 134th Medical Detachment, a unit doing rescue missions for the Special Forces, he completed countless missions in a helicopter, evacuating and treating the wounded, sometimes departing in darkness at 3 a.m.

On July 1, 1964, he was in a Huey helicopter bearing the Red Cross insignia en route to help wounded U.S. forces in a fierce gun battle at Soc Trang in the Mekong Delta, 100 miles south of Saigon. About thirty feet above the ground, the pilot, a major, was mortally wounded by fire coming through the windshield during the intense attack on the helicopter. The helicopter crashed, and Dr. Giles sustained a broken right fibula and a shrapnel wound in his left arm. He dragged the pilot across a field. For the next three hours he used his weapons training to hold off the Viet Cong using a Thompson submachine gun, an M14, and a .45 sidearm. Finally, a combat helicopter came for him and the wounded.

They departed with bullets ricocheting off the helicopter. Dr. Giles returned to Tulane after his tour of duty with the Army. He had multiple medals but he remained humble. I had the privilege of working with him on patients when I was a surgery resident and he was doing his Tulane internal medicine residency. He practiced medicine until recently in Baton Rouge and is now retired. As a result of his war experience, he has a significant hearing disability. As he told me, "You can't wear ear plugs for hearing protection if you want to stay alive." He also said that a lot of what he did was to boost the morale of the wounded on the battlefield by "just being around."

He said the wounded men he met on the battlefield were not afraid of dying. He added that he thinks about his wartime experience a lot.[10]

Sergeant Leonard "Bud" Lomell

For many thousands of American soldiers, June 6, 1944, was a day to make history or a day to die. History was made and many did die.

The day was D-Day. The place was Pointe-du-Hoc, a clifftop location near Omaha Beach on France's Normandy coastline.

The LCA (landing craft assault) was off course. The waves crashed against the boat as it led the way for the greatest armada ever assembled. Gear went overboard. Gunfire riddled the beach and the water. A sister craft sunk and all aboard died except one.

First Sergeant Leonard "Bud" Lomell, of Company D and an original member of the 2nd Ranger Battalion, had a difficult and dangerous mission. Despite the bloody enemy fire aimed at them, he and his Ranger buddies had to scale the looming 100-foot cliff from a rocky beach base thirty yards wide, clustering the troops and making them more susceptible to the heavy fire from enemy troops.

Lomell had a special mission assigned to him if he survived the ascent of the cliff. General Omar N. Bradley, commander of the 1st U.S. Army during the D-Day invasion of Normandy, was to say that Lomell's special assignment was the most difficult mission he had ever given any soldier in his command: Destroy the German cannons that threatened the Allied soldiers on the beaches and the armada taking part in the Normandy invasion.[11]

Survival for Lomell was not a certainty. The Omaha Beach landing site had the highest casualty count of any of the other four sites—Sword Beach, Juno Beach, Gold Beach, and Utah Beach. Of the 4,900 casualties that occurred on D-Day, some 2,400 were at Omaha Beach.

The first wave of men to hit the beach were those of Company A of the 116th Regiment of the Virginia National Guard. As University of New Orleans professor and author Stephen Ambrose pointed out in his book *D-Day, June 6, 1944: The Climactic Battle of World War II*, they were hit by a tremendous barrage of machine-gun and rifle bullets, 88-millimeter and 75-millimeter cannon, exploding mines, mortars, and hand grenades. Ninety percent of the Americans in Company A died there.

Lomell led the way up the cliffs. He was wounded in the ascent, yet continued on his assignment with a fellow Ranger, Sergeant Jack Kuhn, who protected him while he pursued the destruction of the five 155-millimeter cannons threatening the soldiers and the ships in the invasion.

When Lomell reached the place where the aerial photographs had shown what appeared to be cannons, he found instead telephone poles painted black to resemble cannons. He did not give up but instead kept searching and found deep tracks that led him to actual cannons a mile away that had been camouflaged. The German soldiers were nearby. Lomell had to destroy the artillery yet remain undetected. With cover from Kuhn, he crept up to the cannons, used thermite grenades to quietly weld their mechanisms, thus making them inoperable. When he realized that he did not have enough grenades, he made his way back to the other Rangers on the coast road, gathered their grenades, and retraced his perilous journey to the guns. He single-handedly put all of the cannons out of action. He did this while wounded. Thousands of lives were saved because of Lomell's bravery and resourcefulness. En route back to the American lines, Lomell and Kuhn came within twenty feet of 200 German soldiers who were marching across their return path. The two Rangers remained motionless, held their breaths as much as possible, and escaped undetected.

After forty-eight hours of bloody combat, only fifty of the 225 Rangers who landed at Pointe-du-Hoc remained able to fight. The rest were either killed or badly wounded.

To hear Ranger Lomell's voice describe the destruction of the cannons, go to the Web site "Veterans' Chronicles."[12] There you can hear him on an MP3 recording.

But his heroic exploits did not stop with this amazing accomplishment. His Silver Star citation mentions more of his courageous acts on December 7, 1944, at Castle Hill in Germany's Huertgen Forest. It states, in part:

> Conspicuously leading from the front, Lomell directed the successful defense of the hilltop in the face of a nearly overwhelming German counterattack midday. During the German bombardment that preceded the attack, Lomell suffered a head concussion and shrapnel wound in his left arm rendering it useless. Refusing shelter and, at risk of his own life with blood oozing from his ears, nose and mouth, firing his machine gun cradled in his bandaged left arm with his right hand, he continued to lead his men against another ruthless German assault throughout the entire afternoon.[13]

My first meeting with Bud Lomell was in November 2006 at the National World War II Museum in

New Orleans on the occasion of the delayed (because of Hurricane Katrina) celebration of the sixtieth anniversary of the end of war. It was quite a thrill for me because I admired this hero and had spoken of his accomplishments in many of my speeches.

Lomell and I talked again in November of 2007. I asked him what was essential for leadership and he replied, "In a word, honesty. You can't be a good leader and not be honest."

He is a true hero and leader. I can't say it any better than what was said about him when he was awarded an honorary doctor of humanities degree in 2007 by Monmouth University. As Sam Christopher, a reporter at the *Ocean County Observer* wrote, "Lomell was recognized by historian Stephen Ambrose as the single individual, other than Gen. Dwight D. Eisenhower, (responsible) for the success of D-Day on June 6, 1944. While wounded, Lomell, then a 24-year-old Army sergeant, led 200 Army Rangers up the Normandy cliffs under heavy enemy fire."[14]

Lomell received many medals and awards, including the Distinguished Service Cross, Silver and Bronze Stars, the Purple Heart with two clusters, the Croix de Guerre with Silver Lining, the New Jersey Distinguished Service Medal, and the French Legion of Honor, the highest honor one can receive from France, for valor. In talking with him I discovered he also received two high combat medals from England, also praising his bravery.

After my chats with him on two occasions, I found him to be humble, confident, and a wonderful American. When I asked permission to take his photograph, he said: "Sure, but get in the photo with me."[15]

It is a privilege to know Ranger Leonard "Bud" Lomell, American hero, attorney, respected citizen, and a true and outstanding leader of men.

Leadership requires making a decision and taking action. Courage is the fuel for action. Such actions can lead to the making of a hero as in the story of Bud Lomell.

A fascinating painting by artist Larry Selman shows Lomell just after he reached the top of Pointe-du-Hoc.[16]

In chapter 3, I wrote about Audie Murphy and George Washington. They epitomize courage—courage under fire without regard for their own lives. I also told of Wesley Autrey, another hero who risked his life to save another.

One way that true leaders show courage is by actually being in the front of a battle or personally speaking up at a meeting rather than directing from afar or having someone else take the heat for an important issue that may get others upset. Any risk—whether it is gunfire or retaliation at work, or a possible firing for speaking up for truth and ethical behavior—affects them first. Leaders don't put others at risk while remaining safe and hidden.

That display of courage is what inspires loyalty to the leader. One Ranger at Pointe-du-Hoc said he didn't suffer from fear until after he made it to the top of the cliff and saw many of his buddies wounded, and some dying. But then he saw the battalion commander, Colonel James Earl Rudder, being shot but continuing to fight and then saw him blown down by an explosion, yet getting up again to continue fighting. Fear left the Ranger. He would follow Rudder anywhere. That is true inspiration from acts of courage.

Commander (Retired) Paul Galanti

One also can learn about leadership in prisoner of war episodes. A friend, U.S. Navy Commander (Retired) Paul Galanti, was a Navy pilot shot down in Vietnam on his ninety-seventh mission.

On June 17, 1966, while flying an A-4C Skyhawk attack fighter in North Vietnam, Galanti's plane's engine was hit by antiaircraft artillery. The plane was in flames, went out of control, and he had to eject while the plane was going at more than 500 miles an hour. Descending by parachute, Galanti was shot in the neck. Within five minutes of reaching the ground he was captured but not before he sent a radio message and then destroyed the radio. Next was the abusive "Hanoi March." He was forced to walk handcuffed in a parade where he received a soccer kick to his groin that knocked him to the ground. He then spent nearly seven years in North Vietnam's infamous "Hanoi Hilton." He underwent many hours of torture in this prisoner of war camp, but always strove to encourage newly arrived U.S. prisoners despite the risk of punishment for talking or communicating by a tapping code. Galanti wrote me in January of 2008 and said, "I recall telling you in San Francisco in the mid-'90s at dinner at the Penny Farthing Pub on Bush Street how important Admiral Stockdale thought it was to keep us communicating at any cost—up to and including being tortured for trying. He was right." Ironically, when Galanti was walking that night to the hotel after dinner he ran into Admiral Stockdale who had just finished a speech at the Marine Club.

About a year after Galanti was imprisoned, an East German photographer took his photo there. That stark black-and-white image ended up on the cover of *Life* magazine's October 27, 1967, issue. In the photograph Galanti was seated on a bench under a sign reading "Clean Neat." His hands were between his knees and he was "giving the bird" with each of his middle fingers. By the time the photograph made it to the cover of *Life*, the middle fingers had been airbrushed out.[17] He was released from prison February 12, 1973, and he and his wife Phyllis made the February 26, 1973, cover of *Newsweek* when he returned to the United States.[18]

Paul Galanti tells the story of "giving the bird" so everyone would know he was not voluntarily participating in the photo in the transcript of the movie *Return with Honor*.[19]

On February 12, 1998, on the twenty-fifth anniversary of Galanti's release, a cartoon by the late, great Jeff MacNelly, the Pulitzer Prize–winning editorial cartoonist, appeared in the *Chicago Tribune*. It shows a cell door on which is written "Hanoi Hilton" and the door of the cell has broken loose from its hinges. Sunlight is illuminating a wall with these names engraved on it: "Stockdale, Galanti, Stratton, Terry, McCain—ET AL." The caption reads, "25 years ago this month some very good men came home and we're still grateful."

Galanti continues to emphasize the importance of communication in leadership and the responsibility of the leader to teach others how to communicate in adverse conditions as he reminds me in e-mails and reminds others in speeches. Survival is often tied to the ability to communicate. Try to imagine your mental state if you lived for years in solitary confinement in a filthy seven-by-seven-foot cell with a concrete or wood bed. Picture a rusty bucket for a toilet. Rats, geckos, and snakes enter your cell at will. Picture your food, which consists of pumpkin soup plus bread or rice for six months and then a soup of greens plus bread or rice. You lose weight every day and eventually you weigh one hundred pounds, down from a starting weight of 170-plus. That was his experience.

He communicated and taught others the necessity to communicate to maintain sanity and withstand torture, despite the great risks to himself. The punishment for trying to communicate was thirty days in leg irons and being handcuffed behind his back. Despite these hardships, the captors never disrupted communications among the prisoners. Galanti says the communication technique was derived from a Boy Scouts of America Merit Badge effort.

Richard A. Stratton, another U.S. Navy commander held captive in the "Hanoi Hilton," mentions Paul Galanti as the first person to communicate with him in prison:

> I was now a tortured, beaten, starving hulk designated as the "Blackest of Criminals" in the Democratic Republic of Vietnam and an official "Yankee Air Pirate" (eligible to be hung from the yardarm, having been caught in the act of piracy). I was alone, separated from all my shipmates.
>
> I did not know whom to trust. … The walls had more banging and knocking than the whole hull of the venerable 27C that had been my previous home. There was a rhythm and a pattern to the noise that had all the class of a wall full of woodpeckers. I remembered enough Morse code to recognize that

what I was hearing was not Morse code; but it sure wasn't the ghosts of French Foreign Legionnaires having a happy hour. This isolation wing of the prison had a limited number of cells. Once a day you would put your honey bucket out and your morning soup bowl. One of the cells would open up and those prisoners would gather up the gear and proceed to a cell at the end of the passageway that had some running water piped into it. These guys would do the dishes, buckets and their armpits taking their sweet old time, making a hell of a racket and yakking away at each other to beat the band. But wait a minute, they were not talking to each other, they were talking to the rest of us as if they were talking to each other. Each cell had a high barred window open to the air. If you stood on your cement slab pad you could pick up what they were saying.[20]

The following is Galanti's first communication to Stratton. Galanti asks questions and Stratton answers with coughs, one for "yes" and two for "no":

"If you read me, cough once for yes; twice for no."
Cough.
"Are you Air Force?"
Cough. Cough.
"Are you Navy?"
Cough.
"Are you an O-5?"

Cough. Cough.

"Are you an O-4?"

Cough.

"Oh, sh—, another lieutenant commander! Do you know who won the Army-Navy game?"

Cough. Cough.

"Oh hell, a dumb lieutenant commander at that! Jim Stockdale and Robbie Risner [Colonel James Robert Risner] are the SROs (Senior Ranking Officers). Their rules are: communicate at all costs; when they get around to torturing you, hold out as long as you can, bounce back and make them do it all over again; don't despair when they break you, they have broken all of us; pray."

Cough.[21]

TAP CODE CHART

A . .	B . ..	C, K	D	E . .....
F .. .	G	H	I	J .. ..
L	M	N	O	P ... .
Q	R	S	T	U ....
V	W	X	Y	Z ....

[Also see this chart at: http://www.miafacts.org/pages.htm][22]

Galanti continued with a description of the tap code, which uses a matrix of the alphabet, five by five, using "K" and "C" in the same place. For instance, if a prisoner wanted to tap out the letter "O," he'd tap three times, indicating the row, pause and tap four more times, indicating the letter. Galanti explains the rows are remembered by the sentence "American Football League Quits Victorious."

Two Thais are next to you and have been trying to communicate with you. They are using the tap code; it is a box; the first letters are: American Football League Quits Victorious. Communicate. My name is Galanti—Paul Galanti. BANG!

Stratton then goes on to say he heard that loud bang and found out later that the "BANG" was a signal for danger. Paul was hauled out of his cell and tortured. Stratton did not see him for three years. "The rules of the new ball game were quite simple. To lead was to be tortured. To communicate with a fellow prisoner was a de facto sign of leadership resulting in torture. To fail to bow was to be beaten and tortured. To fail to do exactly what you were told and when you were told was to be tortured."[24]

Stratton also says this about Stockdale in a Web posting: "There is an old saying amongst the leaders of troops: 'Never ask your men to do anything that you have not done yourself or would not be willing to do if called upon.' Stockdale lived his orders."[25]

In editorial cartoonist Jeff MacNelly's drawing of the North Vietnam prison, the name at the top of the list carved on the wall is that of Stockdale, who received the Medal of Honor, the nation's highest tribute to its fighting men and women, for his heroism while a captain and POW. The citation accompanying the medal says:

> For conspicuous gallantry and intrepidity at the risk of his life above and beyond the call of duty while senior naval officer in the Prisoner of War camps of North Vietnam. Recognized by his captors as the leader of the Prisoners of War resistance to interrogation and in their refusal to participate in propaganda exploitation, Rear Adm. Stockdale was singled out for interrogation and attendant torture after he was detected in a covert communications attempt. Sensing the start of another purge, and aware that his earlier efforts at self disfiguration to dissuade his captors from exploiting him for propaganda purposes had resulted in cruel and agonizing punishment, Rear Adm. Stockdale resolved to make himself a symbol of resistance regardless of personal sacrifice.
>
> He deliberately inflicted a near-mortal wound to his person in order to convince his captors of his willingness to give up his life rather than capitulate. He was subsequently discovered and revived by the

North Vietnamese who, convinced of his indomitable spirit, abated in their employment of excessive harassment and torture toward all of the Prisoners of War. By his heroic action, at great peril to himself, he earned the everlasting gratitude of his fellow prisoners and of his country. Rear Adm. Stockdale's valiant leadership and extraordinary courage in a hostile environment sustain and enhance the finest traditions of the U.S. Naval Service.[26]

Paul Galanti is the author and webmaster of the popular Nam-POW (Vietnam POWs) site at http://www.nampows.org. His military decorations include the Silver Star, two Legions of Merit for combat, the Meritorious Service Medal, the Bronze Star for combat, nine Air Medals, the Navy Commendation Medal for combat, and two Purple Hearts. The Virginia War Memorial, authorized by the General Assembly of Virginia in 1950 and opened in 1956, has named its new, 17,000-square-foot education center the Paul and Phyllis Galanti Center.[27] On November 12, 2005, Paul Galanti was inducted into the Virginia Aviation Hall of Fame. Over the years, he has remained a keen observer and writer about politics in America. In 2001, thirty-five years after being shot down, Galanti wrote:

I watched in awe as President Reagan rebuilt the country into one that once again was respected and respectable. President Reagan's eight years went by too quickly. Among other things his policies set in motion the greatest economic expansion in our country's history. He rebuilt our military and forced the Communist government in Russia to fold its cards and steal away from the gaming table. He was as popular leaving office as he was coming in— something not seen since the Eisenhower days. He was an anachronistic "straight-shooter" and people loved him for it.[28]

Galanti, a mulitalented individual, is also a motivational speaker. He ends his speeches by saying, "There's no such thing as a bad day when there's a doorknob on the inside of the door," and he always gets a standing ovation.[29]

Senator John McCain

McCain's book *Faith of My Fathers* is a first-person account of what it was like to be a POW in the "Hanoi Hilton" for five and a half years.[30] McCain tells the story in a humble manner, and praises the heroics of his fellow prisoners. He gives evidence that he is not perfect and has made mistakes, but he learned and became a heroic man of many accomplishments. He comes across as an authentic person.

When a wing was blown off McCain's plane by a missile during combat in Vietnam, he ejected while flying over a small lake near Hanoi. His right leg and both arms broke with the ejection. He hit the water. After he reached the shore, a crowd attacked him and an enemy soldier struck him with a rifle, breaking his shoulder. Another stabbed him in the groin and ankle with a bayonet. Just before he was taken away, a woman held tea to his lips as photographers snapped pictures of them.

After he was imprisoned, his weight eventually went down to 100 pounds. To this day McCain cannot lift his arms very high because of the injuries he received during his capture and while being tortured in prison. The lack of medical care made his disability permanent.

He refused early release from prison because he saw this as a public relations maneuver by his captors, as his father was an admiral and commander-in-chief of the Pacific Fleet. McCain said POWs should be released in the order they were captured—first in, first out, complying with the "Code of Conduct for Members of the Armed Forces of the U.S.," which prohibits POWs from seeking special privileges or favors at the expense of fellow POWs.[31]

The North Vietnamese were infuriated at his refusal and broke his ribs, fractured his arm again and knocked teeth out of his mouth.

Senator McCain has this to say in the chapter "Pledge of Allegiance" in *Faith of My Fathers:*

No one who goes to war believes once he is there that it is worth the terrible cost of war to fight it by half measures. War is too horrible a thing to drag out unnecessarily. It was a shameful waste to ask men to suffer and die, to persevere through awful afflictions and heartache, for a cause that half the country didn't believe in and our leaders weren't committed to winning. They committed us to it, badly misjudged the enemy's resolve, and left us to manage the thing on our own without authority to fight it to the extent necessary to finish it. ...

No other national endeavor requires as much unshakable resolve as war. If the government and the nation lack that resolve, it is criminal to expect men in the field to carry it alone. We were accountable to the country, and no one was accountable to us. But we found our honor in our answer, if not our summons."[32]

In an interview on May 14, 1973, with *U.S. News & World Report*, McCain describes his years of solitary confinement: "I remained in solitary confinement ... for more than two years. I was not allowed to see or talk to or communicate with any of my fellow prisoners. My room was fairly decent-sized. I'd say it was about 10 by 10. The door was solid. There were no windows. The only ventilation came from two small holes at the top in the ceiling, about 6 inches by 4 inches. The roof was tin and it got hot as hell in there.

The room was kind of dim night and day, but they always kept on a small light bulb, so they could observe me."[33]

When I was on the American Medical Association board I was returning to New Orleans late one night from Washington, D.C. The flight had few passengers. Because I traveled so much for AMA debating and speaking, I had a lot of frequent flier miles and thus was able to use miles on many occasions to upgrade to first class. On one flight I was seated in a nearly empty first-class section and I saw McCain enter the plane with a man who was on his staff. I said hello as he passed through and continued to the coach section.

I mentioned to the flight attendant that Senator McCain, who was a former POW and a true hero, was in the rear of the plane. I said I was sure the captain would want him moved to first class, especially because so many seats were empty. I gave the flight attendant a note to the captain, and when she returned she said the captain agreed, and that I myself should ask the senator to move up front. I did so, but he declined the invitation. I was impressed with his humility, and later regretted that I hadn't told him how much I admired his courage and service to our country.

• • •

Studying heroes is important in the analysis of leadership. The first question is to determine if the person who acted heroically became a leader implicitly by doing so. Did people willingly follow him or her? Did the hero embody the qualities that I give in my definition of leadership in chapter 3, "The Essentials of Leadership"?

A valid question arises as to whether one can make mistakes or lack the qualities I describe in chapter 3 and still be a leader. My response is that the essentials I gave are the aspirational ideal for the "gold standard" leader. Individuals who performed heroic acts and were chosen to lead are not always perfect. Consider the biblical hero David of Bethlehem, who volunteered to fight the Philistine giant Goliath one-on-one to determine who, between the Israelites and the Philistines, would prevail. After David slays Goliath with a slingshot he beheads him and brings Goliath's head to King Saul, whom David eventually succeeds. David was certainly a hero, but he was not perfect. He slept with Bathsheba, wife of Uriah, and she became pregnant. David subsequently sent Uriah to battle and arranged that he be abandoned during the fight to assure his death.

But King David later found redemption after his and Bathsheba's first child died in infancy. This union subsequently brought forth Solomon whose name immediately brings to mind the phrase "the wisdom of Solomon."

So, as we search for political candidates or others for high-ranking positions in an organization, remember that few individuals will meet all the ideal criteria. The candidates may have made mistakes in the past, but the more important question is whether they learned from them and came to acquire more of the necessary essentials. We do know, nevertheless, that those who acted heroically adhered to principle and acted courageously. Other competitors can only say what they would do in similar circumstances. Heroes have a documented track record.

Lessons Learned

- Leadership is not limited to any one field or walk of life.
- One can learn from the stories of current leaders as well as past ones.
- Heroes do the extraordinary for the benefit of others at great risk to themselves.
- Attitude is enhanced by effective communication and can lead to survival in adverse conditions such as a POW camp.
- In the quest for leaders, seeking out heroes is a good starting point.
- Heroes are not limited to the field of battle.
- In the search for leaders, don't automatically eliminate those who are not perfect.
- Leaders, just as heroes, may have made mistakes in the past. See if they learned and corrected the fault and now warrant redemption and your support.

EPILOGUE

Americans are looking for true leaders. Many people have what it takes to become leaders without recognizing their leadership potential. I've attempted to articulate the essential elements of true leadership so that those who have the capacity to lead might recognize their potential and act on it.

The distinguishing elements of leadership incorporate a proven formula for success. Yet it's also important to understand success in life's work does not make someone a leader. Knowing this makes it easier to separate true leaders from false leaders, who stand to fail during a crisis.

Without the ability to identify true leaders the future is bleak. Disasters, wars, terrorism, and epidemics are just some of the challenges facing the world in the twenty-first century. However, history has shown that leaders frequently emerge during a crisis, and this book presented examples of such leaders as a means of distilling the essence of leadership. Using the criteria presented here, readers will have a much better chance of being able to identify potential leaders. Leadership is not a person's destiny; it is available to everyone who embraces courage, decisiveness, and integrity.

It is everyone's duty to evaluate candidates for
public office and judge them for their potential
for leadership, and then put apathy aside to vote
on Election Day. We must pick individuals based
on their honesty, conviction, and allegiance to the
underpinnings of democracy and liberty. To do less
is a violation of the trust and faith of those who died
giving us our freedoms.

Judge candidates for elective office not only by their
rhetoric but by their past actions. Ask candidates what
their plans are for combating terrorism. Ask what their
plans are for giving everyone access to quality medical
care. Ask if the candidates are for a government run
micromanaged medical system with rationing or for
a system that expands insurance coverage through tax
credits, consumer choice, and market enhancements.
There is a clear difference in these two approaches
and true leaders can defend with evidence the obvious
choice for the best interests of the patients.

I believe Americans are disgusted and apathetic
about the partisanship, patronage and scandals that
continue to stifle progress in Congress. The behavior
in the halls and chambers of Congress also does not
reflect the Declaration of Independence's conclusion:
"And for the support of this Declaration, with a firm
reliance on the protection of divine Providence, we
mutually pledge to each other our Lives, our Fortunes and our sacred Honor." It appears that many

in Congress are not pledging their "Fortunes," but rather working hard to increase their own.

There is no excuse for more death and destruction, as we saw in New Orleans after Hurricane Katrina, because of what I believe to be inept leadership, faulty levee construction and inspections, and lack of preparation for flooding, despite a government mock hurricane two years before that showed what would likely happen. Amid the tragedy of Hurricane Katrina, many stories have surfaced about the heroic rescuers and dedicated medical personnel who stayed behind to care for those trapped in hospitals. No doubt there are more stories to be told. These heroes demonstrated that leaders prepare and make timely decisions to save lives, even if all of the information is not available. To be unprepared when you are given the warning of the high likelihood of disaster is unacceptable. We should have zero tolerance for such behavior. Leaders anticipate what could go wrong and are prepared for it. In the future, let's choose competence over politics.

I frequently use wartime examples of heroism because the risk level for the hero in battlefield situations is almost always death. Courage, heroic acts, and strong leadership qualities obviously are not limited to the battlefield. Volunteers who save lives during disasters are everyday heroes who frequently do not get noticed except by those whose lives they save. These are in addition to the heroic deeds accomplished by other brave people, such as members of the U.S. Coast Guard who risk their lives rescuing those in sinking ships during storms or rescue people on rooftops during floods. Think of all the heroes who rushed to save lives in the horrific terrorist attack on September 11, 2001. Remember the heroic crew and passengers who refused to let the terrorists use United Airlines Flight 93 to destroy a target the terrorists had chosen. They died doing so. Heroes and leaders are everywhere. It's our duty to recognize them. This is the price of freedom. Freedom is not free.

I hope your journey to recognizing, developing, and implementing true leadership abilities is a successful one.

ACKNOWLEDGMENTS

The journey from idea to published book can be a lonely trip, filled with obstacles that appear at first to be insurmountable. But with the generous help of others, what appeared difficult became an exciting challenge.

First on the list is my wife and soulmate, Robin. A skilled attorney, Robin gave up much so I could pursue my dreams. Her unwavering encouragement and love made it possible for me to pursue my dream of this book despite our personal loss from Hurricane Katrina: the destruction of my medical practice and the severe damage to our home. When my outline of the book chapters became convoluted, she went into her best editing mode and gave me a logical path to follow.

Next are my friends at AMA: Dr. Bob Musacchio, Mary Lou White, and Tony Frankos. They made a critical introduction to a legend in the publishing world, Martin Levin, who recommended me to Skyhorse Publishing after reading my book outline and sample chapters.

Once at Skyhorse, President Tony Lyons offered encouragement and gave the manuscript his personal attention. Brando Skyhorse, SVP and assigned editor, was a delight to work with and his suggestions improved the book greatly.

Gene Bourg, who served as editor of our De La Salle high school newspaper where I was a columnist, resumed his editorial duties in reviewing my manuscript prior to submission to Skyhorse. His editorial suggestions come from a forty-year career at a daily newspaper and were invaluable.

Raymond French, a dear friend since high school who deserves a chapter for his accomplishments in the aerospace industry, modestly deferred mention and instead suggested that I share the story of John C. Houbolt, the person responsible for the lunar orbital rendezvous concept in America's successful moon landing in 1969. Raymond also made sure that I understood and depicted the engineering concepts accurately.

Much appreciation is due to all of the leaders I had the privilege to interview. They shared their personal experiences and gave their perspective on true leadership. I am in the debt of those who read the manuscript and offered for publication their comments about the book. Governor Bobby Jindal, a very busy man, deserves special thanks for finding time to write the foreword for this book.

Finally, any success in life that I have enjoyed has been because of the sacrifices and opportunities my parents gave me. Dad was a heroic policeman who taught me life's lessons not only by his words, but also by his actions. Mom, ninety-four years young at the time of her death in 2008, impressed upon me that civility is not a sign of weakness, long before President Kennedy said it in his inaugural speech.

NOTES

Chapter 1: The Antithesis of Leadership

1. http://www.noaanews.noaa.gov/stories2006/ s2656.htm (Accessed March 28, 2008). http://www.nws.noaa.gov/os/assessments/pdfs/ Katrina.pdf (Accessed March 28, 2008).

2. Mayor Nagin Ray Nagin, interview, *Meet the Press*, NBC, September 11, 2005. Transcript at: http://www.msnbc.msn.com/id/9240461/ (Accessed March 11, 2008).

3. Mike Brown, interview by Paula Zahn, *Paula Zahn Now*, CNN, September 1, 2005. See: http://transcripts.cnn.com/TRANSCRIPTS/0509/01/ pzn.01.html (Accessed March 11, 2008).

4. Hurricane Pam hypothetical hurricane exercise discussion of July 20, 2004 at: http://www. ohsep.louisiana.gov/archive/incaseofemergency exercise.htm (Accessed March 11, 2008).

5. FEMA discusses Hurricane Pam in press release July 23, 2004 at: http://www.fema.gov/news/ newsrelease.fema?id=13051 (Accessed March 11, 2008).

6. Congressional Reports: H. Rpt. 109-377, *A Failure of Initiative: Final Report of the Select Bipartisan Committee to Investigate the Preparation for and Response to Hurricane Katrina*, http://www.gpoaccess.gov/serialset/creports/katrina.html (Accessed March 11, 2008). See "bureaucratic inertia was causing death" in executive summary at: http://a257.g.akamaitech.net/7/257/2422/15feb20061230/www.gpoaccess.gov/katrina report/execsummary.pdf (Accessed March 12, 2008).

7. *The Times-Picayune*, November 29, 2007.
8. *The Times-Picayune*, December 16, 2005.
9. *The Times-Picayune*, November 17, 2007.

Chapter 3: The Essentials of Leadership: Success Cornerstones and More

1. http://www.ushistory.org/valleyforge/washington/george2.html (Accessed March 29, 2008); Harlow Giles Unger, *The Unexpected George Washington—His Private Life* (New Jersey: John Wiley & Sons, Inc., 2006) 28.

2. Paul Davis, "Calling All Soldiers: A Charge from General George Washington," http://ezinearticles.com/?Calling-All-Soldiers:-A-Charge-from-General-George-Washington&id=349262 (Accessed March 29, 2008).

3. http://poe.house.gov/News/DocumentSingle. aspx?DocumentID=56387 (Accessed March 28, 2008).

4. http://www.medalofhonor.com/MedalOf HonorAudieLMurphy.htm (Accessed March 29, 2008).

5. Philip Washburn, "American WWII Hero Makes Famous One-Man Stand," *Fort Hood Sentinel*, January 23, 1997.

6. "Details about the daring subway track rescue," Gothamist.com, January 3, 2007, http://gothamist.com/2007/01/03/details_about_t.php (Accessed March 29, 2008).

7. "Hero Saves Man Who Fell on Subway Tracks," WINS Radio, New York, NY January 2, 2007, http://www.1010wins.com/pages/166150.php?contentType=4&contentId=276869 (Accessed March 31, 2008).

Chapter 4: A Primer on "Homework"

1. Etiology of Cholera is at World Health Organization. See: http://www.who.int/topics/cholera/control/en/ (Accessed March 13, 2008).

2. http://en.wikipedia.org/wiki/London (Accessed March 12, 2008).

3. John Snow, MD, *On the Mode of Communication of Cholera* (London: John Churchill, New Burlington Street, 1855).

4. Ibid., 38–40 and http://www.ph.ucla.edu/epi/snow/removal.html (Accessed March 29, 2008).

5. John Snow, MD, *On the Mode of Communication of Cholera* (London: John Churchill, New Burlington Street, 1855).

6. Except from the Lancet editorial. See: http://www.ph.ucla.edu/epi/snow/reactionand committeeaction.html (Accessed March 12, 2008).

7. *Brain Research Bulletin*, Vol. 38, No. 2, 161–165, 1995 accessed at: http://www.ph.ucla.edu/epi/snow/brainresearchbul38(2)_161_165_1995.pdf and http://www.ph.ucla.edu/EPI/snow/first discoveredcholera.html (Both accessed March 11, 2008).

8. http://www.ph.ucla.edu/epi/snow/death.html (Accessed March 11, 2008).

9. http://www.au.af.mil/au/awc/awcgate/navy/skelton_whispers.htm (Accessed March 12, 2008).

10. Ibid.

11. PubMed can be accessed at: http://www.ncbi.nlm.nih.gov/sites/entrez?db=pubmed (Accessed March 12, 2008).

12. http://www.lib.berkeley.edu/TeachingLib/Guides/Internet/SearchEngines.html (Accessed March 12, 2008).

13. Ibid.

14. National Cancer Institute at: http://www.cancer. gov/cancertopics/pdq/treatment/breast/patient (Accessed March 12, 2008).

15. Mayo Clinic page on breast cancer: http://www. mayoclinic.com/health/breast-cancer/DS00328/ DSECTION=7 (Accessed March 13, 2008).

Chapter 5: Courage

1. http://www.theodoreroosevelt.org/research/ speech%20kill%20moose.htm (Accessed March 29, 2008).

2. *Detroit Free Press*, October 15, 1912. See: http:// www.historybuff.com/library/refteddy.html (Accessed March 12, 2008).

3. Theodore Roosevelt, "Man in the Arena," speech at the Sorbonne, Paris, April 23, 1910. See: http:// www.theodore-roosevelt.com/trsorbonnespeech. html (Accessed March 13, 2008).

4. Viscount Lee of Fareham, English statesman. See: http://www.theodoreroosevelt.org/life/biotr. htm (Accessed March 13, 2008).

5. Robert F. Kennedy, foreword to *Profiles in Courage*, Memorial Edition (New York: HarperCollins Publishers, Inc., 1964) 9.

6. John Fitzgerald Kennedy, *Profiles in Courage*. (New York: HarperCollins Publishers, Inc., 1955) 225.

7. http://www.cdc.gov/ncidod/EID/vol7no2/ cover.htm (Accessed March 13, 2008); http:// en.wikipedia.org/wiki/Ignaz Semmelweis (Accessed March 13, 2008).

8. Jurgen Thorwald, *The Century of the Surgeon* (New York: Pantheon Books, Inc., 1957) 223–226. See also: http://en.wikipedia.org/wiki/Gustav_ Adolf_Michaelis; (Accessed March 13, 2008).

9. Nick Bacon and John Hawk, interview by the Congressional Medal of Honor Foundation, *Medal of Honor: Portraits of Valor Beyond the Call of Duty* (Artisan, 2003)

10. http://www.brainyquote.com/quotes/authors/l/ leonardo_da_vinci.htm (Accessed March 29, 2008).

11. www.gatesfoundation.org (Accessed March 13, 2008). Listing of AMA's Nathan Davis award winners was at: http://www.ama-assn.org/ama/ pub/category/3353.html (Accessed January 1, 2008) but that link no longer is active and AMA's Web site editor confirmed on March 13, 2008 that "AMA Web site does not maintain content in perpetuity; rather, it has an expiration date and then it is deleted." However, the Web site editor sent what previously was at the link:
Ms. Patty Stonesifer, President of the Bill & Melinda Gates Foundation accepted the award and the following citation.
"The recipient of the 2001 Outstanding Global Health Initiative is the Bill & Melinda Gates

Foundation Global Health Program. This Seattle-based organization is recognized for its contributions worldwide on children's health, vaccine development, reproductive health, and disease eradication. The Foundation has funded hundreds of millions of dollars for life-saving vaccines that will protect children against respiratory, diarrheal and liver diseases, as well as disabling diseases such as polio. The Foundation has helped countless people of all ages battle HIV/AIDS, tuberculosis, malaria, cervical cancer, measles, African sleeping sickness and more. Donald J. Palmisano, MD, JD, of Metairie, Louisiana, nominated the Gates Foundation for this award."

12. Melinda French Gates, June 25, 2007, written message to Dr. Palmisano.

13. http://thinkexist.com/quotation/courage_is_ grace_under_pressure/144972.html (Accessed March 13, 2008).

14. Lewis Millet, interview by Congressional Medal of Honor Foundation, *Medal of Honor*.

Chapter 6: Persistence: "Don't Give Up!"

1. According to Bartleby, "attributed to Calvin Coolidge. Unverified, though this appeared on the cover of the program of a memorial service for him in 1933. The Forbes Library, Northampton,

Massachusetts, has searched its Coolidge collection many times for this." See http://www.bartleby.com/73/1355.html (Accessed March 31, 2008).

2. Landing a man on the moon was proposed in a "Special Message to the Congress on Urgent National Needs" by President John F. Kennedy before a joint session of Congress May 25, 1961. The speech can be found at: http://www.jfklibrary.org/Historical+Resources/Archives/Reference+Desk/Speeches/JFK/003POF03NationalNeeds05251961.htm (Accessed March 31, 2008). Also, for the political circumstances at the time of that decision, see: http://history.nasa.gov/moondec.html (Accessed March 31, 2008).

3. James R. Hansen, *Enchanted Rendezvous: John C. Houbolt and the Genesis of the Lunar-Orbital Rendezvous Concept.* See http://www.hq.nasa.gov/office/pao/History/monograph4/splash2.htm (Accessed March 12, 2008); http://www.hq.nasa.gov/office/pao/History/monograph4/crusade.htm (Accessed March 12, 2008).

4. *The Journey to the Moon* at http://www.thekeyboard.org.uk/The%20journey%20to%20the%20Moon.htm (Accessed March 12, 2008).

5. http://www.hq.nasa.gov/office/pao/History/monograph4/crusade.htm (Accessed March 31,

2008). Also see note 32 at: http://www.hq.nasa.
gov/office/pao/History/monograph4/notes.
htm#32 (Accessed March 31, 2008).

6. http://www.hq.nasa.gov/office/pao/History/
monograph4/against.htm (Accessed March 31,
2008).

7. http://history.nasa.gov/monograph4/seaman.
htm (Accessed March 31, 2008).

8. http://history.nasa.gov/monograph4/conclude.
htm (Accessed March 31, 2008).

9. Transcript of words heard on Earth is at:
http://www.buffalostate.edu/documents/
moonlanding.pdf (Accessed March 31, 2008);
An analysis of the words spoken and the documentation of the missing "a" preceding "man"
is at: http://www.chron.com/disp/story.mpl/
front/ 4225856.html (Accessed March 31,
2008).

10. See note 8.

Chapter 7: Decisiveness

1. Chet Huntley, "B-52 crashes at Ellsworth, South
Dakota AFB," *NBC Evening News*, Friday, Apr
03, 1970.

2. George Canning, 1770–1827, British Statesman. See http://www.character-in-action.com/
character-quotes/decisiveness.htm (Accessed
March 12, 2008).

Chapter 8: Communication

1. http://www.wisdomquotes.com/002173.html (Accessed March 12, 2008).

2. Complete text of debate is at: http://www.debates.org/pages/trans88c.html (Accessed March 12, 2008).

3. William Strunk, Jr., and E.B. White, *The Elements of Style*, 3rd ed. (New York: Allyn and Bacon, 1979), 23.

4. Marie L. Waddell, Robert M. Esch, and Roberta R. Walker, *The Art of Styling Sentences: 20 Patterns to Success*, (New York: Barron's Educational Series, Inc., 1972), 24

5. Text and audio of President Kennedy's Inaugural Address are at: http://www.jfklibrary.org/Historical+Resources/Archives/Reference+Desk/Speeches/JFK/003POF03Inaugural01201961.htm (Accessed April 1, 2008).

6. Dr. Martin Luther King, Jr., "I Have a Dream" speech, http://www.mlkonline.net/sounds.html (Accessed April 1, 2008).

7. Lucile Vaughan Payne, *The Lively Art of Writing*, (Chicago: Follett Publishing Company, 1965) 124.

8. Edmond Rostand, *Cyrano de Bergerac*, trans. Brian Hooker (New York: Bantam Books, 1971), 76.

9. Robert Friedman, "Effective Speechwriting," lecture at the American Medical Association's

National Leadership Conference in Los Angeles March 9–12, 2002. This was the third year of similar lectures by Mr. Friedman that Dr. Palmisano attended. On March 30, 2002, Dr. Palmisano wrote Mr. Friedman and said in part: "The famous advertising great, David Ogilvy, once wrote, 'When Aeschines spoke, they said, "How well he speaks." But when Demosthenes spoke, they said, "Let us march against Philip." This reminds me of you.'" On December 20, 2007, Dr. Palmisano talked with Mr. Friedman and got his permission to print excerpts from his lectures.

10. http://www.americanrhetoric.com/top100 speechesall.html (Accessed March 12, 2008).
11. http://www.bartleby.com/124/pres43.html (Accessed April 1, 2008).
12. See note 5 this chapter.
13. http://www.museum.tv/archives/etv/K/htmlK/ kennedy-nixon/kennedy-nixon.htm (Accessed March 12, 2008).
14. http://www.history.org/almanack/life/politics/ giveme.cfm (Accessed April 1, 2008).

Chapter 9: Creativity and Acquiring the State of Mind Necessary for Success

1. Donald J. Palmisano, "The 20-Year Anniversary of the Louisiana Medical Malpractice Act of 1975, 'Act 817 of 1975': A Tribute to John

C. Cooksey, MD." *Journal of the Louisiana State Medical Society* 147: (11) (1995): 481–4.

2. Donald J. Palmisano, "A Quest For Justice Against the Wrongful Medical Malpractice Suit: Louisiana's Unique Advantage." *Loyola Law Review*, 27, No. 2, (1981); Donald J. Palmisano, "Countersuits Key Strategy Against Wrongful Suits." *American Medical News,* September 17, 1982.

3. http://en.wikipedia.org/wiki/Tim_Berners-Lee (Accessed March 12, 2008).

4. http://www.livinginternet.com/i/ii_arpanet. htm; http://en.wikipedia.org/wiki/ARPANET (Both accessed March 12, 2008).

5. http://en.wikipedia.org/wiki/ASCII (Accessed March 12, 2008).

6. For a discussion of computer communication protocols, see: http://www.rentron.com/Myke7. htm (Accessed March 12, 2008).

7. Donald J. Palmisano, "Louisiana's Medical Malpractice Laws: A Rescue From Danger", *AMA State Health Legislation Report*, 12, No. 4, November 1984.

8. http://econdevleader.blogspot.com/2007/03/ edward-de-bono-creativity-vital-to.html (Accessed March 12, 2008).

9. http://www.wanderings.net/notebook/Main/ NewThinkByEdwardDeBono. (Accessed March 12, 2008).

10. http://www.brainyquote.com/quotes/authors/e/edward_de_bono.html (Accessed March 12, 2008).

11. The story, paraphrased, comes from Edward DeBono, *New Think: The Use of Lateral Thinking in the Generation of New Ideas*. (New York: Basic Books, 1967).

12. Roger von Oech, *A Whack On The Side of The Head: How to Unlock Your Mind for Innovation*, (New York: Warner Books, 1983); Roger von Oech, *A Kick in the Seat of the Pants: Using Your Explorer, Artist, Judge, and Warrior to be More Creative* (New York: Harper and Row, 1986).

13. http://www.creativethink.com (Accessed March 12, 2008); http://blog.creativethink.com/2006/ 12/my_favorite_new.html (Accessed April 1, 2008).

14. Regarding Thomas Edison light bulb research, see: http://www.ushistory.net/electricity.html; http://www.pbs.org/wgbh/amex/edison/filmmore/description.html (Both accessed March 12, 2008).

Chapter 10: Interpersonal Relationships

1. http://www.rc.umd.edu/rchs/reader/ozymandias.html (Accessed April 2, 2008).

2. http://www.kipling.org.uk/poems_if.htm (Accessed April 2, 2008).

Chapter 11: Finding Truth

1. To obtain a copy of the *Beyond Blame* video go to the online store of Institute for Safe Medication Practices at: http://onlinestore.ismp.org/catalog.cfm?catid=3 (Accessed March 12, 2008).

2. Joint Commission Internet address for Sentinel Events is: http://www.JointCommission.org/SentinelEvents/SentinelEventAlert; See also http://www.pubmedcentral.nih.gov/articlerender.fcgi?artid=1117775. For more discussion of the connectors and latent errors and human factors; see article from *British Medical Journal*, 2000 March 18; 320 (7237): 785–788; see Institute of Safe Medication Practices at http://www.ismp.org/Newsletters/acutecare/articles/20041216_2.asp to learn of other connector errors by searching connector error. (All accessed March 11, 2008.)

3. Donald J. Palmisano, "Why Your Doctor Might Quit," *The Saturday Evening Post*, November/December 2004 issue, Volume 276, Number 6; See also Donald J. Palmisano, "The Hidden Cost of Medical Liability Litigation," *The Annals of Thoracic Surgery, 2004;78:9–13*. It can be viewed online at: http://ats.ctsnetjournals.org/cgi/reprint/78/1/9.pdf. (Accessed March 11, 2008).

4. http://www.pubmedcentral.nih.gov/articlerender.fcgi?artid=1123321 (Accessed April 2, 2008). Also see Susan Mayor, "Researchers claim clinical trials are reported with misleading statistics,"

British Medical Journal, June 8, 2002; 324(7350): 1353.

5. The value of statistics and the misuse of statistics can be found at: http://hoa.aavso.org/ (Accessed March 11, 2008).

6. See "How to understand statistics" at: http://www.bbc.co.uk/dna/h2g2/A1091350; as well as: http://www.robertniles.com/stats; http://www.robertniles.com/stats/tests.shtml; http://www.socialresearchmethods.net/selstat/ssstart.htm; http://www.graphpad.com/www/Book/Choose.htm; http://en.wikipedia.org/wiki/Misuse_of_statistics; http://www.pubmedcentral.nih.gov/articlerender.fcgi?artid=1123321; British Medical Journal, 2002 June 8; 324(7350): 1353; http://hoa.aavso.org/mathtalk.htm; For the Mark Twain quote, http://en.wikipedia.org/wiki/Lies,_damned_lies,_and_statistics, *The Autobiography of Mark Twain*. See http://www.amazon.com/Autobiography-Mark-Twain-Perennial-Classics/dp/0060955422. (All accessed March 11, 2008.)

Chapter 12: Financial Considerations and Fiduciary Responsibility

1. Randy Zeller's comments obtained by e-mail on January 28, 2008.

2. http://www.conference-board.org (Accessed March 12, 2008); http://en.wikipedia.org/wiki/

The_Conference_Board (Accessed March 12, 2008.); http://aicpa.org (Accessed March 12, 2008).

3. Dave Preimesberger comments obtained by e-mail on December 7, 2007.

4. This talented financial expert taught me much about financial analysis over the years. She answered my questions by e-mail on January 24, 2008 and modestly elects not to have her name mentioned.

5. http://www.investopedia.com/terms/c/contributionmargin.asp (Accessed March 12, 2008); http://en.wikipedia.org/wiki/Contribution_margin (Accessed March 12, 2008); http://www.investopedia.com/terms/f/freecashflow.asp (Accessed March 12, 2008).

6. Daniel L. Kurtz, *Board Liability: Guide for Nonprofit Directors*, (New York: Moyer Bell Limited, 1988), 21.

7. Ibid., 28–29.

Chapter 13: Expanding Your Horizons

1. http://www.ushistory.org/paine/crisis/c-01.htm (Accessed April 15, 2008).

2. Donald Phillips, *The Founding Fathers On Leadership—Classic Teamwork in Changing Times* (New York: Warner Books, 1977), 64.

3. Houston Peterson, ed., *50 Great Essays* (New York: Pocket Books, 1954).
4. Michael S. Lief, H. Mitchell Caldwell, Ben Bycel, *Ladies and Gentlemen of the Jury, Greatest Closing Arguments in Modern Law* (New York: Scribner, 1998), 29–57; see also Robert H. Jackson's complete summation to the court at the University of Missouri-Kansas City School of Law: http:// www. law.umkc.edu/faculty/projects/ftrials/nuremberg/ Jacksonclose.htm (Accessed March 11, 2008).

Chapter 14: Putting Information Technology to Use

1. Roger Ebert, in *Yahoo! Internet Life*, September, (1998): 66; http://marylaine.com/exlibris/cool. html (Accessed March 11, 2008).
2. Verlyn Klinkenborg, "Trying to Measure the Amount of Information That Humans Create," *The New York Times*, November 12, 2003.
3. http://en.wikipedia.org/wiki/Exabyte (Accessed March 11, 2008).
4. http://datacenterjournal.com/index. php?option=com_content&task=view&id= 934&Itemid=40 (Accessed March 12, 2008 but requires registration to access).
5. http://www.hds.com/products/storage-systems/ content-archive-platform. (Accessed March 11, 2008).

Chapter 16: Some Leaders You May Never Have Heard of (and Some You Have)

1. The biography of Dr. Zhu Chen for his inaugural article is in the Proceedings of the National Academy of Sciences of the United States of America at: http://www.pnas.org/cgi/content/full/101/15/5325 (Accessed April 2, 2008). From this Web site one can access the inaugural article entitled "All-trans retinoic acid/As_2O_3 combination yields a high quality remission and survival in newly diagnosed acute promyelocytic leukemia."

2. Telephone interview with Dr. Bagian December 28, 2007 and e-mail correspondence of January 1, 2008.

3. E-mail reply October 3, 2007 with Bobby Jindal's definition of leadership.

4. E-mail correspondence from Dr. Anderson to Dr. Palmisano on January 4, 2008.

5. http://www.huffingtonpost.com/phillip-k-howard/judgesshould-take-back-t_b_52193.html (Accessed March 12, 2008).

6. Richard Deichmann, *Code Blue: A Katrina Physician's Memoir* (Indiana: Rooftop Publishing, 2007).

7. Annis, Edward. 1993. *Code Blue: Health Care In Crisis* (Washington, D.C.: Regnery Publishing, 1993); a review of Dr. Annis's book is at: http://

www.haciendapub.com/codeblue.html.   Also
read *Time* magazine's accouns of Dr. Annis in
1962 at: http://www.time.com/time/magazine/
article/0,9171,940022,00.html (Accessed March
11, 2008); and again in *Time* magazine May 11,
1962 at: http://www.time.com/time/magazine/
article/0,9171,939359,00.html (Accessed March
11, 2008). Dr. Annis reminded Dr. Palmisano
that after Medicare was passed, despite the law
prohibiting any government interference, all of
his predictions came true. Note that the law
specifically prohibited federal interference yet
it happens every day in the Medicare program.
When the law was passed, it said:

*Prohibition Against Any Federal
Interference*

SEC. 1801. [42 U.S.C 1395] Nothing in this
title shall be construed to authorize any Federal
officer or employee to exercise any supervision
or control over the practice of medicine or the
manner in which medical services are provided
or over the selection, tenure, or compensation
of any officer or employee of any institution,
agency, or person providing health service; or
to exercise any supervision or control over the
administration or operation of any such institution, agency, or person.

Obviously the federal government did not follow that law. Dr. Annis's prophecy came to past. The government soon required pre-admission approval by bureaucrats looking at a checklist. That was a flop.

Then in 1997 the government prohibited balance billing for any fees not covered by the government. If the patient opts out of the Medicare program and pays the physician the amount both agree the service is worth, the physician is not allowed back into the Medicare program for two years. And almost every year physicians are threatened by Congress with a reduction in payment under a "Sustainable Growth Rate" formula. See http://www.cbo.gov/ftpdocs/75xx/doc7542/09-07-SGR-brief.pdf (Accessed April 2, 2008) for the government's description of this complex formula that is tied to the gross domestic product. In 2007 the proposed reduction was ten percent. When it costs more to deliver a service than you are paid for it, the service stops being delivered. No surprise with that conclusion. As Henry Hazlitt states in his classic book, *Economics in One Lesson*, you have to consider the long-term effect of a decision and not just the immediate result. With Medicare and its unworkable formula, the short-term effect is saving money and the long-term effect is physicians reduce the number of Medicare patients they treat because physicians cannot balance bill for the true cost of the service. The citizens suffer with this micromanagement and central control.

Here is what is printed in the journal *Health Affairs* in an article entitled "What Medicare's Architects Had In Mind," by Robert M. Ball, who served a commissioner of Social Security under Presidents Kennedy, Johnson, and Nixon,

> In fact, the first section of Title XVIII of the Social Security Act providing for health insurance for the elderly was a "Prohibition Against any Federal Interference … or over any institution, agency or person providing health services."
>
> We soon found that this prohibition had to be interpreted narrowly. We did have to interfere, but the provision illustrates where we started.

The article goes on to say "Medicare now pays about 10 percent less than its fair share to hospitals and perhaps a third under market rates to physicians." See Robert M. Ball, "What Medicare's Architects Had In Mind," *Health Affairs*, Volume 14, Number 4; http://content.healthaffairs.org/cgi/reprint/14/4/62.pdf (Accessed April 2, 2008).

For the perspective of the federal government of the events in 1962, see: http://www.ssa.gov/history/corningchap4.html (Accessed April 2, 2008). Now Section 4507 of BBA 97 authorizes physicians and patients to privately contract with patients but only if the physician agrees not to accept any Medicare payments for any Medicare beneficiary for at least two years. See: Duke Center for Health Policy and Management, http://www.hpolicy.duke.edu/cyberexchange/Regulate/CHSR/HTMLs/P1-Medicare%20Assignment%20Rules.htm (Accessed March 12, 2008).

Dr. Palmisano believes the solution for Medicare and other government medical programs is to allocate money by tax credits or vouchers to those who need help getting insurance and give them an array of choices of insurance. Also, the uninsured problem can be solved by expanding insurance coverage through tax credits, consumer choice, and market enhancements. The patient is in control and if the patient doesn't like the amount of money allocated, the patient contacts Congress. The hallmark of the free enterprise system is the right to privately contract. Congress violates that principle with Medicare and other government medical programs. To continue in the same federal programs ultimately will result in loss of access to care for patients.

See Donald J. Palmisano, David W. Emmons, Greg D. Wozniak, "Expanding insurance coverage through tax credits, consumer choice, and market enhancements: the American Medical Association proposal for health insurance reform," *Journal of the American Medical Association* (May 12, 2004) 291(18):2237–42.

8. Interview recording November 12, 2007; E-mail to Dr. Palmisano, Friday, November 23, 2007; see praise of Dr. Annis at page 51 of minutes of AMA June 2003 meeting containing Dr. Palmisano's inaugural speech (47–52) at: http://www.ama-assn.org/meetings/public/annual03/calltoorder.pdf (Accessed March 12, 2008); also posted at http://www.hcmsdoctors.org/politics/AMA%20Updates/Inaugural%20Address%20of%20Dr.%20Donald%20Palmisano.htm (Accessed March 12, 2008).

9. E-mail to Dr. Palmisano, July 24, 2007.

10. Interview January 23, 2008 at home of Dr. Giles.

11. http://www.historynet.com/magazines/world_war_2/3029731.html (Accessed March 12, 2008).

12. Leonard Lomell, interview by Veterans' Chronicles, MP3 recording at: http://www.wwiivets.com/veteransaudioandvideo/Veteran%27s%20Chronicles/Leonard%20Lomell%20and%20Jack%20Kuhn%20.mp3;

For additional information see: http://www.militaryhistoryonline.com/wwii/articles/pointeduhoc.aspx (Accessed March 12, 2008).

13. Leonard Lomell Silver Star Citation at: http://www.rotary7500.org/newsletter_files/Boots'Bits%20Newsletter%20Nov.pdf (Accessed April 2, 2008).

14. http://timesbeacon.com/apps/pbcs.dll/article?AID=/20071109/NEWS/711090304/1/SPORTS06 (This link no longer is active but Dr. Palmisano has the article in his files. In trying to find the information at other Web sites, one cannot help but find much information on the Internet about Leonard Lomell including this additional discovery from *Time* magazine, March 31, 2003, at: http://www.time.com/time/magazine/article/0,9171,1004504,00.html [Accessed March 13, 2008]).

15. Dr. Palmisano interview and correspondence with Leonard "Bud" Lomell in 2006 and 2007.

16. Painting also featured at http://www.valorstudios.com/RangersAtThePoint.htm(Accessed March 12, 2008); *The Point* by Larry Selman, copyright 2006 featuring Ranger hero Leonard Lomell at Pointe-du-Hoc D-Day June 6, 1944 is featured in this book with artist's permission.

17. Paul Galanti in "Hanoi Hilton" infamous prison camp at: http://www.nampows.org/life.jpg (Accessed March 12, 2008).

18. Another photo of Galanti, this one of him and his wife on his return to the U.S., appeared on the cover of *Newsweek*'s February 23, 1973, issue. That image can be seen at http://www.worldnetdaily.com/images2/newsweekgalanti.jpg (Accessed March 12, 2008); his military history is located at: http://www.pownetwork.org/bios/g/g046.htm (Accessed March 12, 2008).

19. *Return with Honor* film transcript at: http://www.pbs.org/wgbh/amex/honor/filmmore/pt.html (Accessed March 12, 2008).

20. "The Boat School Boys" by Richard A. Stratton is at: http://www.axpow.org/boatschoolboys.htm (Accessed March 12, 2008).

21. Ibid.

22. Communication tap chart at: http://www.miafacts.org/pages.htm (Accessed March 12, 2008).

23. See citation 21.

24. Ibid.

25. http://www.aiipowmia.com/inter22/in040802ww2.html (Accessed March 12, 2008).

26. Read Medal of Honor Citation and see photos of Rear Admiral Stockdale in "Hanoi Hilton" at: http://www.medalofhonor.com/JamesStockdale.htm (Accessed March 12, 2008).

27. http://www.vawarmemorial.org/ (Accessed March 12, 2008).

28. http://www.pownetwork.org/bios/g/g046.htm (Accessed March 12, 2008).

29. Multiple e-mail communications and interviews with Paul Galanti from November 5, 2007, to January 17, 2008.

30. John McCain with Mark Salter, *Faith of My Fathers* (New York: Random House, 1999).

31. http://www.b-29s-over-korea.com/book_reports/The-John-McCain-Story01.html (Accessed March 12, 2008); see also: http://ethics.iit.edu/codes/coe/dept.defense.code.fighting.force.html (Accessed March 12, 2008).

32. John McCain with Mark Salter, *Faith of My Fathers* (New York: Random House, 1999), 334–335.

33. "How the POWs Fought Back," See http://www.freerepublic.com/focus/f-news/1084711/posts (Accessed March 12, 2008).

INDEX